Enhancing
AGRICULTURAL INNOVATION

Enhancing
AGRICULTURAL
INNOVATION

How to Go Beyond the
Strengthening of Research Systems

THE WORLD BANK
Washington, DC

©2007 The International Bank for Reconstruction and Development / The World Bank
1818 H Street NW
Washington DC 20433
Telephone: 202-473-1000
Internet: www.worldbank.org
E-mail: feedback@worldbank.org

1 2 3 4 5 11 10 09 08 07

This volume is a product of the staff of the International Bank for Reconstruction and Development / The World Bank. The findings, interpretations, and conclusions expressed in this volume do not necessarily reflect the views of the Executive Directors of The World Bank or the governments they represent.

The World Bank does not guarantee the accuracy of the data included in this work. The boundaries, colors, denominations, and other information shown on any map in this work do not imply any judgement on the part of The World Bank concerning the legal status of any territory or the endorsement or acceptance of such boundaries.

ISBN-10: 0-8213-6741-2   eISBN: 0-8213-6740-4
ISBN-13: 978-0-8213-6741-4   DOI: 10.1596/978-0-8213-6741-4

Library of Congress Cataloging-in-Publication Data

Enhancing agricultural innovation : how to go beyond the
strengthening of research systems.
    p. cm. — (Agriculture and rural development)
  Includes bibliographical references.
  ISBN-13: 978-0-8213-6741-4
  ISBN-10: 0-8213-6741-2
  ISBN-10: 0-8213-6740-4 (electronic)
  1. Agricultural innovations—Case studies. I. World Bank. II.
Series: Agriculture and rural development series.
  S494.5.I5E575 2006
  338.1′6—dc22   2006031508

Photos: Corbis (cover); Arne Hoel, World Bank Photo Library (interior)
Cover design: Patricia Hord Graphik Design

CONTENTS

BOXES, FIGURES, AND TABLES

Boxes

Figures

Tables

PREFACE

This book, originally a World Bank Economic and Sector Work paper, was initiated as a result of the international workshop, "Development of Research Systems to Support the Changing Agricultural Sector," which was organized by the Agriculture and Rural Development Department of the World Bank in June 2004 in Washington, DC. One of the main conclusions of the workshop was that "strengthened research systems may increase the supply of new knowledge and new technologies, but such strengthening may not necessarily correlate very well with the capacity to innovate and adopt innovations throughout the agricultural sector, and thereby with economic growth." This paper uses an innovation systems perspective to explore which other interventions may be required.

The innovation systems concept is not new. It has been applied in other sectors, mainly in industry. The concept is considered to have great potential to add value to previous concepts of agricultural research systems and growth by (1) drawing attention to the totality of actors needed for innovation and growth, (2) consolidating the role of the private sector and stressing the importance of interactions within a sector, and (3) emphasizing the outcomes of technology and knowledge generation and adoption rather than the strengthening of research systems and their outputs.

Although the innovation systems concept has raised interest within the agricultural sector, the operational aspects of the concept remain largely unexplored. At the same time, within and outside the World Bank, agricultural investment strategies have gone through a number of changes, some of which are closely related to the innovation systems concept. This paper takes stock of real-world innovation systems and assesses the usefulness of the innovation systems concept for guiding investments in agricultural technology development and economic growth.

The paper incorporates prior innovation systems work and eight new case studies of innovation systems, plus potential investments to support their development. The manuscript has been produced through a fruitful collaboration between the World Bank's Agriculture and Rural Development Department, its South Asia Agriculture and Rural Development Department, and the United Nations University–Maastricht Economic and Social Research and Training Centre on Innovation and Technology (UNU-MERIT).

EXECUTIVE SUMMARY

Investments in knowledge—especially in the form of science and technology—have featured prominently and consistently in most strategies to promote sustainable and equitable agricultural development at the national level. Although many of these investments have been successful, the context for agriculture is changing rapidly, sometimes radically.

Six changes in the context for agricultural development heighten the need to examine how innovation occurs in the agricultural sector:

1. Markets, not production, increasingly drive agricultural development.
2. The production, trade, and consumption environment for agriculture and agricultural products is growing more dynamic and evolving in unpredictable ways.
3. Knowledge, information, and technology increasingly are generated, diffused, and applied through the private sector.
4. Exponential growth in information and communications technology has transformed the ability to take advantage of knowledge developed in other places or for other purposes.
5. The knowledge structure of the agricultural sector in many countries is changing markedly.
6. Agricultural development increasingly takes place in a globalized setting.

Can new perspectives on the sources of agricultural innovation yield practical approaches to agricultural development that may be more suited to this changing context? That is the central question explored here.

CHANGING APPROACHES FOR SUPPORTING AGRICULTURAL INNOVATION

As the context of agricultural development has evolved, ideas of what constitutes "research capacity" have evolved, along with approaches for investing in the capacity to innovate:

- In the 1980s, the "national agricultural research system" (NARS) concept focused development efforts on strengthening research supply by providing infrastructure, capacity, management, and policy support at the national level.
- In the 1990s, the "agricultural knowledge and information system" (AKIS) concept recognized that research was not the only means of generating or gaining access to knowledge. The AKIS concept still focused on research supply but gave much more attention to links between research, education, and extension and to identifying farmers' demand for new technologies.
- More recently, attention has focused on the *demand* for research and technology and on the development of *innovation systems,* because strengthened research systems may increase the supply of new knowledge and technology, but they may not necessarily improve the capacity for innovation throughout the agricultural sector.

THE INNOVATION SYSTEMS CONCEPT

An *innovation system* can be defined as a network of organizations, enterprises, and individuals focused on bringing new products, new processes, and new forms of organization into social and economic use, together with the institutions and policies that affect their behavior and performance. *The innovation systems concept embraces not only the science suppliers but also the totality and interaction of actors involved in innovation.* It extends beyond the creation of knowledge to encompass the factors affecting demand for and use of knowledge in novel and useful ways.

The innovation systems concept is derived from direct observations of countries and sectors with strong records of innovation. The concept has been used predominantly to explain patterns of past economic performance in developed countries and has received far less attention as an operational tool. It has been applied to agriculture in developing countries only recently, but it appears to offer exciting opportunities for understanding how a country's agricultural sector can make better use of new knowledge and for designing alternative interventions that go beyond research system investments.

AIM OF THIS PAPER

This paper seeks to assess the usefulness of the innovation systems concept in guiding investments to support the development of agricultural technology. To that end, it develops an operational agricultural innovation systems concept for the Bank's client countries and collaborators. This paper does not challenge the importance of investing in science and technology capacity, which is well recognized in innovation systems theory. Rather, it focuses on the *additional insights* and *types of interventions* that can be derived from an innovation systems perspective and that can influence the generation and use of science and technology for economic development.

METHODOLOGY

Three key tasks were undertaken to assess the utility of the innovation systems concept and develop an operational framework:

1. Developing an analytical framework for the innovation systems concept.
2. Applying the analytical framework in eight case studies and conduct a comparative analysis of the results.
3. Using the results of the analysis, developing an intervention framework for assessing innovation systems (consisting of a typology of innovation and other diagnostic features) and for identifying potential interventions (based on guiding principles and examples).

The Analytical Framework

The four main elements of the analytical framework are (1) key actors and their roles, (2) the actors' attitudes and practices, (3) the effects and characteristics of patterns of interaction, and (4) the enabling environment for innovation.

The Comparative Analysis

Four criteria were used to select case studies that would capture elements of the dynamic agricultural context: (1) niche sectors that have shown strong patterns of growth, (2) sectors that have been strongly integrated into global markets, (3) traditional sectors that are being transformed by the growth of activities further up the food chain and that can highlight implications of the industrialization of the food chain, and (4) sectors that provide large employment opportunities for the poor. The eight case studies included medicinal plants and vanilla production in India; food processing and shrimp production in Bangladesh; cassava processing and pineapple production in Ghana; and cassava processing and cut flower production in Colombia.

A conceptual framework was developed to facilitate the comparative analysis of innovation systems in these eight settings. A number of tools were applied to explore partnerships and organizations. An important additional tool was a checklist for *conducting diagnostic assessments* in the eight settings and for *developing interventions* based on an innovation systems framework.

The checklist was designed to address a central insight of the innovation systems framework: partnerships and linkages must be analyzed in their historical and contemporary context, which greatly defines the *opportunities* and *necessities* for innovation, especially where rapid change is occurring. The context includes policy, market, and trade conditions and the challenges they present, as well as other contextual factors, such as the sociopolitical environment and the natural resource base. A description of the changing context reveals any divergence between the innovation system and its practices on the one hand and the changing demands imposed by the context on the other. The checklist includes the following major issues:

- *Actors, the roles they play, and the activities in which they are involved,* with an emphasis on diversity of public and private sector actors and on the appropriateness of their roles.
- *Attitudes and practices of the main actors,* with an emphasis on collaboration, potential inefficiencies, patterns of trust, and the existence of a culture of innovation.
- *Patterns of interaction,* with an emphasis on networks and partnerships, inclusion of the poor, and the existence and functions of potential coordination and stakeholder bodies.
- *Enabling environment (policies and infrastructure),* with an emphasis on the role of policies related to science, technology, and fiscal concerns; the role of farmer and other organizations in defining research and innovation challenges; and the significance of legal frameworks.

The Intervention Framework

The intervention framework, derived from the case study analysis, departs from many earlier uses of the innovation system concept by providing additional guidance on diagnosis (the most common use of the concept) and by adding specific ideas for interventions to develop the capacity of innovation systems. The framework has four elements: (1) *a typology of agricultural innovation environments,* which helps the user rapidly assess the characteristics of an innovation system in a particular context; (2) *diagnostic features* for each phase of innovation system development, which help explain why certain features are likely to impede innovation and identify promising arrangements that could be built upon; (3) *principles for intervention,* based on the diagnostic features; and (4) *options for intervention,* based on the case study examples.

KEY FINDINGS FROM THE INNOVATION CAPACITY ANALYSIS

The analysis of innovation capacity in the eight settings studied revealed the following:

1. Linkages for creating dynamic systems of innovation frequently have been absent.
2. Attitudes and practices are a major obstacle to innovation. Strong incentives to innovate, arising from exposure to highly competitive markets, have rarely been sufficient to induce new patterns of collaboration.
3. The lack of interaction results in limited access to new knowledge, weak articulation of demand for research and training, weak or absent technological learning, weak or absent organizational learning at the company/farmer/entrepreneur level and at the sector level, weak sector upgrading, weak integration of social and environmental concerns into sector planning and development, and weak connections to sources of financing for innovation.
4. Challenges are evolutionary, continuous, always changing, and integrated.
5. The major characteristics of innovation across the case studies are as follows:
   - Innovation is neither science nor technology but the application of knowledge of all types to achieve desired social and economic outcomes.
   - Often innovation combines technical, organizational, and other sorts of changes.
   - Innovation is the process by which organizations "master and implement the design and production of goods and services that are new to them, irrespective of whether they are new to their competitors, their country, or the world" (Mytelka 2000).
   - Innovation comprises radical and many small improvements and a continuous process of upgrading.
   - Innovation can be triggered in many ways.
   - Considerable value is being added in nontraditional agricultural sectors.

TOWARD A FRAMEWORK FOR INNOVATION SYSTEM DIAGNOSIS AND INTERVENTION

Different Development Trajectories

The process of innovation is shaped in very different ways, depending on the particular context in which innovation systems emerge and how this context changes over time. First, the pivotal actors that start the process are different—broadly speaking, they are either public or private actors. Second, the factors that trigger innovation are quite different—they may be either policy or market triggers. These initial conditions tend to shape two distinct innovation trajectories or systems: an *orchestrated trajectory* and an *opportunity-driven trajectory*.

Orchestrated innovation systems have several phases of development:

- A *pre-planned phase,* in which no research or other policy intervention has been made, as new opportunities have not yet been identified. Many developing countries are at this stage.

- In the *foundation phase*, priority sectors and commodities have been identified, and the government supports them through research and policy interventions. However, these efforts often have a limited effect on growth.
- In the *expansion phase*, the government intervenes with projects and special programs to link actors in the innovation system.

Opportunity-driven innovation systems have several phases of development:

- The *nascent phase* resembles the pre-planned phase of orchestrated systems but the private sector is more proactive. Companies or individual entrepreneurs have identified new market opportunities, but a recognizable sector has yet to emerge. Many of the case study sectors began in this way.
- In the *emergence phase*, the sector takes off. Rapid growth is observed, driven by the activity of the private sector or nongovernmental organizations (NGOs). The sector starts to be recognized by the government.
- In the *stagnation phase*, the sector faces increasing and incremental evolutionary pressures to innovate because of competition, particularly from other countries, and because of changing consumer demands and trade rules. This situation is the most common across the case studies.

The ultimate phase of development in orchestrated and opportunity-driven systems is a *dynamic system of innovation*, which can be established with the right type of support. The sector is neither publicly nor privately led but characterized by a high degree of public and private interaction and collaboration in planning and implementation. It is agile, responding quickly to emerging challenges and opportunities and delivering economic growth in socially inclusive and environmentally sustainable ways.

Intervention Options

The innovation systems concept places great emphasis on the context-specific nature of arrangements and processes that constitute a capacity for innovation. For this reason, *principles of intervention* rather than *prescriptions* are emphasized here. Interventions in advanced phases of development typically can build on interventions from earlier phases; the more advanced the phase, the more varied the interventions that can take place simultaneously.

- *Initiating interventions* (for example, building trust or improving the ability to scan and reduce risk for new opportunities) allow the transition from the pre-planned phase to the foundation phase.
- *Experimental interventions* (for example, supporting partnerships on emerging opportunities, or developing attitudes, practices, and financial incentives) allow the transition from the foundation phase to the expansion phase.

- *Interventions that help build on or nurture success* (for example, expanding proven initiatives, strengthening good practices, and addressing weaknesses) allow the transition from the expansion or emergence phase to a dynamic system of innovation.
- *Remedial interventions* (for example, building coherence and links between the research system and the sector, supporting coordination bodies, and strengthening or redesigning existing organizations) help resolve the weaknesses of innovation capacity in the stagnation phase.
- *Maintenance interventions* (for example, maintaining agility and the ability to identify new opportunities and challenges, enhancing collaboration across actors and sectors, and contributing to the maintenance of an enabling environment) are aimed at ensuring that dynamic systems of innovation do not deteriorate.

CONCLUSIONS

Key Findings

Nine key findings emerge on the nature of innovation and innovation capacities:

1. Research is an important component—but not always the central component—of innovation.
2. In the contemporary agricultural sector, competitiveness depends on collaboration for innovation.
3. Social and environmental sustainability are integral to economic success and must be reflected in interventions.
4. The market is not sufficient to promote interaction—the public sector has a central role to play.
5. Interventions are essential for building the capacity and fostering the learning that enable a sector to respond to continuous competitive challenges.
6. The organization of rural stakeholders is a central development concept. It is a common theme in innovation systems development and in numerous agricultural and rural development efforts.
7. Actors that are critical for coordinating innovation systems at the sector level are either overlooked or missing.
8. A wide set of attitudes and practices must be cultivated to foster a culture of innovation.
9. The enabling environment is a key component of innovation capacity.

Utility of the Innovation System Concept

The assessment of the innovation systems concept and the intervention framework yields the following observations:

1. Through its explicit attention to development outcomes, the innovation systems concept offers a new framework for analyzing both the roles of science and technology and their interaction with other actors to generate goods and services.
2. The innovation systems concept can be very effective in identifying the missing links in traditional sectors and potentially improving the innovation dynamics. This dynamism often depends on the presence of some sectorwide coordinating capacity for identifying innovation challenges and pursuing novel approaches to innovation.
3. The application of the innovation systems concept in agricultural development requires additional empirical validation. In this respect, the analysis described here has contributed to a learning process, similar to the process proposed for building innovation capacity in a sector.
4. Universally applicable blueprints for innovation system development do not exist. Development practitioners must be willing to work with emerging concepts and must recognize that the interventions they are planning will evolve while they learn.
5. The innovation systems concept promotes the integration of poverty and environment issues into sector development planning by altering the roles and interactions of actors in the public sector, the business community, and civil society.
6. The concept provides a framework for inclusive, knowledge-intensive agricultural development, but more experience is required before the contours of a truly pro-poor, pro-environment, and pro-market innovation system can be fully defined.

Contributions to the Design of Development Interventions

In conclusion, the innovation systems concept makes the following contributions to designing development interventions:

- Interventions should not focus first on developing research capacity and only later on other aspects of innovation capacity. Instead, research capacity should be developed in a way that from the beginning nurtures interactions between research, private, and civil society organizations.
- The analysis reveals the possibility of linking up with previous efforts at capacity development. Recent discussions of innovation capacity have argued that capacity development in many countries involves two sorts of tasks. The first is to create networks of scientific actors around research themes such as biotechnology and networks of rural actors around development themes such as dryland agriculture. The second is to build links between these networks so that research can be used in rural innovation. A tantalizing possibility is that interventions that unite research-based and community-

based capacity could cost relatively little, add value to existing investments, result in pro-poor innovation capacity, and achieve very high returns.

Implications for the World Bank

What are the implications for the World Bank?

- *With respect to research and extension,* the Bank should increasingly look to what it wants to achieve, not to what it wants to support. Support for research systems must focus more on developing the interface with the rest of the sector. This effort will require that major attention be given to improving research system governance and to strengthening the ability to form partnerships. The Bank should support investments that foster pluralism in service providers and that have the ability to find the right approach and mix of partners in different innovation systems contexts.
- *With respect to agricultural education,* an effective innovation system requires a cadre of professionals with a new skill set and mindset. Technical expertise needs to be complemented with functional expertise in (for example) markets, agribusiness, intellectual property law, rural institutions, and rural finance, which will place strong demands on educational systems. The Bank should reengage in efforts to modernize curricula, support staff training, and develop distance learning and other facilities.
- *For support of agricultural sector development in general,* this paper emphasizes the importance of developing the agricultural sector's institutional infrastructure. The Bank must support more institutional innovation efforts in addition to more traditional technology-oriented research, especially in poor countries, because new ways of doing business have often been central to success.
- *Regarding the Bank's position in the dialogue on agricultural development at the global and national levels,* this paper suggests that the Bank should facilitate the development of a stronger global community of practice in the field of agricultural innovation. A final concrete step is to collect further experiences from work by the Bank and other agencies to develop operational information on the alternative interventions that have been proposed.

ACKNOWLEDGMENTS

This paper was prepared by Andy Hall (United Nations University– Maastricht Economic and Social Research and Training Centre on Innovation and Technology), Willem Janssen (Task Team Leader, SASAR), Eija Pehu (ARD), and Riikka Rajalahti (ARD). The task team extends thanks to Paul Engel (ECDPM), Ponniah Anandajayasekeram (IFPRI-Addis Ababa), Barbara Adolph (NRI), Vandana Chandra (PREMED), Animesh Shrivastava (ARD), Indira Ekanayake (LCSER), and Derek Byerlee (AFTS2) for helpful comments on the concept note and the manuscript. Their contributions are highly appreciated.

Lynn Mytelka and Banji Oyeyinka of UNU-MERIT are recognized for their support in developing the methodology. The team would also like to thank Erwin de Nys and Jonathan Agwe (ARD) for their input into the paper and Kelly Cassaday for editing, formatting, and incorporating textual revisions into the manuscript. The team appreciates the considerable contributions of Lynn Mytelka, Rasheed Sulaiman V., Muhammad Taher, Isabel Bortagaray, George Essegbey, and Zahir Ahmed in carrying out the country case studies and expresses its appreciation to Ekin Keskin for background reviews of trends in agriculture.

The task team would also like to recognize the support and guidance of Kevin Cleaver (Director, ARD) and Sushma Ganguly (Sector Manager, ARD). In addition the team thanks Constance Bernard (Director, SASAR) and Gajanand Pathmanathan (Sector Manager, SASAR) for supporting the cooperation between SASAR and ARD that made this study possible. Special thanks go to Melissa Williams and Marisa Baldwin for their inputs in the cover design, logistics, and production of the book; Catherine Ragasa for managing the final revisions; Kathy Kelly for copyediting; and Aziz Gökdemir, Patricia Katayama, and Nora Ridolfi of the World Bank's External Affairs–Office of the Publisher (EXTOP) for managing the final production and publication of the book. Finally, the team wishes to acknowledge the financial contribution of DFID and the assistance of Neil Macpherson in arranging the DFID support.

ACRONYMS AND ABBREVIATIONS

AFTS2	Eastern Africa—Economic and Social Sustainable Development (World Bank)
AIN	Agricultural Investment Note
AKIS	agricultural knowledge and information system
APEDA	Agricultural and Processed Food Products Export Development Authority
APROYSA	Association of Small-Scale Cassava Farmers from the Cordoba and Socre Plains
ARD	Agriculture and Rural Development (World Bank)
ASCo	Ayensu Starch Company Limited
Asocolflores	Colombian Association of Flower Exporters
ATMAs	agricultural technology management agencies
BRAC	Bangladesh Rural Advancement Committee
CDD	community-driven development
CIAT	Centro Internacional de Agricultura Tropical (International Center for Tropical Agriculture)
CIMMYT	International Maize and Wheat Improvement Center
CLAYUCA	Consorcio Latinoamericano y del Caribe de Apoyo a la Investigación y al Desarrollo de la Yuca (Latin American Consortium for Cassava Research and Development)

COFUPRO	national coordinating agency
CONACYT	National Council on Science and Technology
CORPOICA	Colombian Corporation for Agricultural Research
DFID	Department for International Development (U.K.)
ECDPM	European Center for Development Policy Management (World Bank)
EU	European Union
EurepGAP	Global Partnership for Safe and Sustainable Agriculture
FAO	Food and Agriculture Organization (of the UN)
FFPED	Forum for Food Processing Enterprise Development
FRLHT	Foundation for the Revitalisation of Local Health Traditions
GAP	Good Agricultural Practices
GTZ	German Agency for Technical Cooperation
HACCP	Hazard Analysis Critical Control Point (regulation)
IAP	Innovative Activity Profile
ICAR	Indian Council on Agricultural Research
ICT	information and communications technology
IFPRI	International Food Policy Research Institute
INIFAP	national agricultural research organization
LCSER	Latin America and Caribbean—Agriculture and Rural Development (World Bank)
NAIS	national agricultural innovation system
NARS	national agricultural research system
NGO	nongovernmental organization
NRI	Natural Resources Institute
OECD	Organisation for Economic Co-operation and Development
PREMED	Poverty Reduction and Economic Management—Economic Policy and Debt (World Bank)
R&D	research and development
SASAR	South Asia Agriculture and Rural Development (World Bank)
SUCICP	Sustainable Uptake of Cassava as an Industrial Commodity Project
USAID	U.S. Agency for International Development
WTO	World Trade Organization

CHAPTER ONE

Reasons for Assessing the Value of the Innovation Systems Perspective

KNOWLEDGE GENERATION AND APPLICATION IN A CHANGING AGRICULTURAL CONTEXT

Agricultural development depends to a great extent on how success-fully knowledge is generated and applied. Investments in knowledge—especially in the form of science and technology—have been featured prominently and consistently in most strategies to promote sustainable and equitable agricultural development at the national level. Although many of these investments have been quite successful (box 1.1), the context for agriculture is changing rapidly—sometimes radically—and the process of knowledge generation and use has been transformed as well (box 1.2). It is increasingly recognized that traditional agricultural science and technology investments such as research and extension, although necessary, are not sufficient to enable agricultural innovation. As this paper will demonstrate, new perspectives on the nature of the agricultural innovation process can yield practical approaches to agricultural development that may be more suited to this changing context.

The Changing Context of Agricultural Development

Six changes in the context of agricultural development heighten the need to examine how innovation occurs in the agricultural sector.

First, markets—not production—increasingly drive agricultural development. For most of the 20th century, major progress in agricultural development was inextricably linked to major improvements in the productivity of staple food

Box 1.1   Past Contributions of Science and Technology

The historical focus of research on food crop technologies, especially genetic improvement of food crops, has undeniably been successful. Average crop yields in developing countries have increased by 71 percent since 1961, while average grain yields have doubled (to 2.8 tons per hectare). Yields of many commercial crops and livestock have also grown rapidly (see figure). International Food Policy Research Institute (IFPRI) studies on impacts of public investment in India and China showed that agricultural research and development had higher impacts on poverty reduction compared to most other public investments, second only to investment in education in China and in rural roads in India (Fan, Zhang, and Zhang 2002; Fan, Hazell, and Thorat 1999). Other studies have shown that a 1 percent increase in agricultural yields in low-income countries leads to a 0.8 percent reduction in the number of people below the poverty line (Thirtle, Lin, and Piesse 2003).

Yield Growth in Developing Countries; 1961–2001

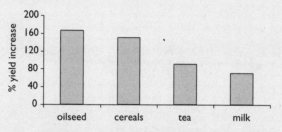

Source: World Bank 2006a; FAOSTAT 2002.

Box 1.2   The Changing Process of Knowledge Generation and Use

From:	To:
■ The knowledge elite	■ The knowledge society
■ Paper used to store and share knowledge	■ Digital media and the Web used to store and share knowledge
■ Research as the key tool to generate knowledge	■ Research and consultation to generate knowledge
■ The linear model: research knowledge adaptation use of technology	■ The interactive model: innovations arise from a learning-based process that combines problem recognition and knowledge generation

crops, but this situation is changing. With falling staple food prices and rising urban incomes, the payoff has shifted to strategies that enhance agricultural diversification and increase the value added of agricultural production (Barghouti et al. 2004). Despite their past prominence in driving agricultural development, centralized public research systems are finding it difficult to cater to this trend.

Second, the production, trade, and consumption environment for agriculture and agricultural products is increasingly dynamic and evolving in unpredictable ways. If farmers and companies are to cope, compete, and survive in contemporary agriculture, they need to innovate continuously. Drivers for innovation include, for example, emerging health and disease problems such as avian flu and HIV/AIDS; changing patterns of competition in local and, in particular, global markets; changing trade rules and the need for continuous upgrading to comply with them; and changing technological paradigms, such as biotechnology and information technology and the opportunities and challenges that they present.

Third, knowledge, information, and technology are increasingly generated, diffused, and applied through the private sector. Private businesses develop and supply a substantial number of the technologies that farmers use or introduce (examples include seed, fertilizer, pesticides, and machinery). The role of the private sector is expected to grow with the increasing intensification of agriculture.

Fourth, exponential growth in information and communications technology (ICT), especially the Internet, has transformed the ability to take advantage of knowledge developed in other places or for other purposes (Arnold and Bell 2001). Both the ICT and the biotechnology revolutions have driven home the fact that many innovations within the agricultural sector—examples include geographic information systems, global positioning systems, and bioinformatics—are based on knowledge generated in other sectors. The question of how to take advantage of new knowledge has become just as urgent as the question of how to generate and diffuse new knowledge.

Fifth, the knowledge structure of the agricultural sector in many countries is changing markedly. Thirty years ago, the number of people with postgraduate degrees was very small, and the number of uneducated farmers and farm workers was in the hundreds of millions. Under these circumstances, it made perfect sense to create a critical mass of intellectual resources in a few places, mostly in national agricultural research institutes, to generate new technologies. Since then, overall and agricultural education levels have increased in many countries. Greater numbers of experienced and educated people—in the farm community, the private sector, and nongovernmental organizations (NGOs)—now interact to generate new ideas or develop responses to changing conditions. Technical change and innovation have become much more interactive processes, which can be led by many different types of actors (Janssen and Braunschweig 2003).

Sixth, agricultural development increasingly takes place in a globalized setting. This change affects all of the five changes mentioned previously: the domestic market is not the only market that defines demand, environmental and health issues cross the borders of any country, knowledge from abroad may be more important than domestically generated knowledge, and ICT allows information to spread through internationally organized networks of practitioners. Globalization causes quality standards to be defined increasingly by international markets and leads small sectors suddenly to confront huge potential demand. It raises the stakes in agricultural development: success, for example, in the export of nontraditional products may assume larger dimensions than in a more insular world, but failure to adapt to new conditions will also have larger consequences and may cause traditional trade patterns to erode rapidly.

Innovation Trends in Agricultural Production Systems

Most agricultural production is increasingly integrated in value chains with forward (marketing) and backward (input supply) linkages. Urban markets often cause supply chains to grow longer; in turn, shelf life, handling requirements, and other market requirements assume greater importance for agricultural products. Before reaching the consumer, traditional staples such as wheat or rice may pass through the hands of several agents (assembly agent, miller, wholesaler, retailer, and baker), and more value may be added in the food processing stage than in production. New bulk or niche markets may appear, such as the animal feed market for maize (box 1.3) and cassava or the soluble fiber market for oats. Agricultural production is increasingly based on a wider range of purchased (or free) inputs—seed, fertilizer, pesticides, machinery, and water—that must be combined and used judiciously to arrive at sustainable production systems. Each of the links in these "production-to-consumption" systems provides new opportunities for innovation.

The issues surrounding agriculture have changed in tandem with these changes in production. For example, poverty may be reduced more rapidly by creating employment along the value chain than by increasing production on the farm. Concern over food safety may influence input use and postharvest management more than cost. Labor and water productivity may be as important as (or more important than) land productivity. Public health threats such as mad cow disease and avian influenza have triggered public interventions on a scale more often evoked by famines or natural disasters. Other public health issues include nutritional concerns related to deficiencies of major or minor nutrients and to obesity. Everywhere—in developing as well as developed countries—the convenience of food consumption and preparation is becoming as important as the price of food (Maxwell and Slater 2003).

The traditional food sectors in developing countries are not insulated from these developments. Many show signs of rapid transformation. At the market end, the options for utilizing cassava and maize have expanded to include ani-

India's research efforts since the Green Revolution have focused on rice and wheat. Yields of maize—considered an inferior, coarse grain—remained low.

Recently the outlook for maize in India has been transformed as rising incomes, an expanding population, accelerating urbanization, and declining prices have pushed the demand for poultry to unheard-of levels. Broiler production grew by 12 percent per annum during 1995–2003. Because maize is the main ingredient for poultry feed, demand for maize grew along with the poultry industry.

The exploding demand for maize-based feed was accompanied by major policy reforms that facilitated private sector participation. The New Policy for Seed Development, enacted in 1988, changed licensing policies to encourage investment from domestic and multinational seed companies. The subsequent 1991 Industrial Policy, which identified seed production as a priority investment, further facilitated multinationals' entry into India's seed market.

Companies responded quickly. By 1998, an estimated 218 private domestic companies and 10 multinationals were supplying maize seed to India. Many had their own hybrid breeding programs. Yields of the newly available hybrids are comparable to yields worldwide, and maize production has grown to 13 million tons.

Source: Naik 2006.

mal feed, starch, and fructose. Demand for dairy and meat products has grown very rapidly (often at 5 percent or more per year), stimulated by new hygiene and public health management requirements as well as greatly increased product differentiation (cheese, yogurt, yogurt drinks, cream, fluid milk, cold meats, prepared meals, and myriad other products). At first glance, the rice and wheat sectors may seem less dynamic, but quality considerations and the differentiation of production by end use (for example, grain, bread, or cake) increasingly present opportunities for innovation. In all cases, the transformation of traditional food sectors through marketing may be accompanied by equally strong transformation on the production side. New approaches are required to respond adequately to the opportunities and threats that these transformation processes offer (World Bank 2005).

Changing Approaches for Supporting Agricultural Innovation

As the context of agricultural development has changed, ideas of what constitutes innovation have changed, and so have approaches for investing in it (box 1.4). In the 1980s, the concept of the "national agricultural research system," or NARS,[1] was developed to guide investments in agricultural development. Development activities based on the NARS concept generally focused on strengthening research supply by providing infrastructure, capacity, management, and policy support at the national level. In the 1990s, the "agricultural knowledge and information system" (AKIS)[2] concept gained currency. The AKIS concept recognizes that research is not the only means of generating or gaining access to knowledge. Although the AKIS concept also focuses on research supply, it gives much more attention to the links between research, education, and extension and the identification of farmers' demand for new technologies.

Strengthened research systems may increase the supply of new knowledge and new technologies, but they may not necessarily improve the capacity for innovation throughout the agricultural sector (Rajalahti, Woelcke, and Pehu 2005). Recently more attention has been given to the demand for research and technology and to the development of wider competencies, linkages, enabling attitudes, practices, governance structures, and policies that allow this knowledge to be put into productive use. The concept of an innovation system has guided this more holistic approach to planning knowledge production and use. This paper uses this concept to develop a framework for guiding the diagnosis of innovation capacity and for planning interventions.

An *innovation system* may be defined as comprising the organizations, enterprises, and individuals that together demand and supply knowledge and

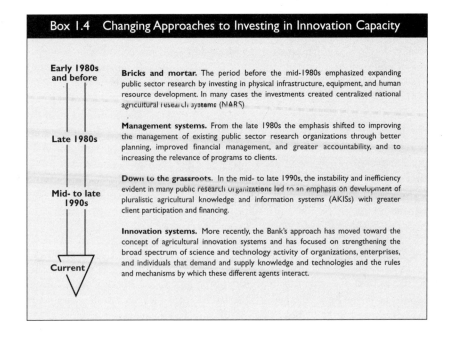

Box 1.4   Changing Approaches to Investing in Innovation Capacity

Early 1980s and before

Bricks and mortar. The period before the mid-1980s emphasized expanding public sector research by investing in physical infrastructure, equipment, and human resource development. In many cases the investments created centralized national agricultural research systems (NARS)

Late 1980s

Management systems. From the late 1980s the emphasis shifted to improving the management of existing public sector research organizations through better planning, improved financial management, and greater accountability, and to increasing the relevance of programs to clients.

Mid- to late 1990s

Down to the grassroots. In the mid- to late 1990s, the instability and inefficiency evident in many public research organizations led to an emphasis on development of pluralistic agricultural knowledge and information systems (AKISs) with greater client participation and financing.

Current

Innovation systems. More recently, the Bank's approach has moved toward the concept of agricultural innovation systems and has focused on strengthening the broad spectrum of science and technology activity of organizations, enterprises, and individuals that demand and supply knowledge and technologies and the rules and mechanisms by which these different agents interact.

Figure 1.1   A Stylized Innovation System

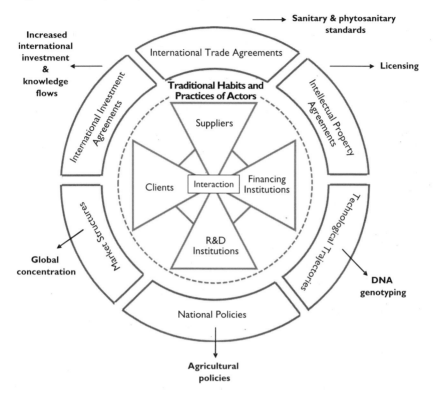

Source: Adapted from Mytelka 2000.

technology, and the rules and mechanisms by which these different agents interact. The innovation systems concept focuses not merely on the science suppliers but on the totality and interaction of actors involved in innovation. It extends beyond the creation of knowledge to encompass the factors affecting demand for and use of new and existing knowledge in novel and useful ways. Thus, innovation is viewed in a social and economic sense and not purely as discovery and invention. Figure 1.1 presents a stylized innovation system and the context in which it might operate.

The innovation systems concept is attractive not only because it offers a holistic explanation of how knowledge is produced, diffused, and used but also because it emphasizes the actors and processes that have become increasingly important in agricultural development. To recapitulate some of the points made earlier, agricultural development plans are no longer concerned almost exclusively with staple food production. These plans now give far more attention to diversifying into new crops, products, and markets and to adding value to serve new markets better (Barghouti et al. 2004). These changes are driven by rapid urbanization and by the increased integration of many developing countries into global markets for agricultural products and services. This market-led agricultural development relies more strongly on the private sector and on the interaction of agriculture with other sectors and disciplines. Because new markets for agricultural products and services change continuously, agricultural development depends more than ever on a process of continuous, incremental innovation. The scope of innovation includes not only technology and production but also organizations (in the sense of attitudes, practices, and new ways of working), management, and marketing changes, therefore requiring new types of knowledge not usually associated with agricultural research and new ways of using this knowledge. Ways of producing and using knowledge must also adapt and change. The innovation systems concept emphasizes adaptive tendencies as a central element of innovation capacity.

TOWARD OPERATIONAL AGRICULTURAL INNOVATION SYSTEMS

The innovation systems concept appears to offer exciting opportunities for understanding how a country's agricultural sector can make better use of new knowledge and can design alternative interventions that go beyond research investments. The concept is robust: its principles are derived from direct observations of countries and sectors with strong track records of innovation, although most of these observations come from developed countries and the industrial sector. To date, the concept has been used predominantly to explain past patterns of economic performance. It has received far less attention as an operational tool for diagnosing the capacity of a sector for generating and using knowledge and for designing interventions to strengthen weaknesses in innovation capacity. It has been applied to agriculture in developing countries only recently (Hall et al. 2001; Hall 2005). Traditionally, public policy and donor assistance, including assistance from the World Bank, have focused on building capacity and providing operational funds for research and technology transfer systems.

The question then is whether the principles and insights arising from the innovation systems concept, and the perspective on innovation capacity development that it implies, can be converted into operational tools for policies and projects that address the practical challenges of agricultural development and sustained economic growth. This paper attempts to answer that question. It assesses the usefulness of the innovation systems concept in guiding investments to support the development of agricultural technology, and it develops an operational agricultural innovation systems concept for the Bank's client countries and its collaborators.

This paper does not challenge the importance of investing in research capacity, which is well recognized in the innovation systems concept as an important element of innovation capacity. Rather, it focuses on the *additional insights* and *types of interventions* that can be gained from an innovation systems perspective.

GROUNDING THE INNOVATION SYSTEMS CONCEPT IN THE "NEW AGRICULTURE"

Although staple food production will remain very important, an exciting agricultural trend in many countries is the rapid emergence of many new production-to-consumption systems. Agricultural sectors around the world are increasingly diversifying into vegetables and fruits, spices, aquaculture products, and nonfood products (such as medicinal plants and cut flowers); the production of animal protein is increasing; and the importance of postharvest handling and processing is growing to meet (mostly urban) consumers' demand for storability and convenience (CGIAR Science Council 2005). These new agricultural activities are highly volatile, but frequently they provide considerable income and employment opportunities. Their development can make a large contribution to rural-based sustainable development.

Many of these new agricultural activities and products emerge when private entrepreneurs respond to new market opportunities. Often the production and marketing efforts for these new products are quite sophisticated. Although the overall value of new agricultural activities can be considerable, the large number of products makes it impossible to develop national research programs for each one, except perhaps in very large countries such as China and India. Consequently, countries must develop new approaches to support innovation in these knowledge-intensive activities.

This "new agriculture" provides many suitable case studies for developing an operational framework based on the agricultural innovation systems concept, because it typifies several important new patterns in the agricultural sectors of many developing countries:

- The delineation of new, dynamic, and very knowledge-intensive niche sectors, such as export horticulture and agroprocessing.
- Rapid evolution in production, consumption, and marketing conditions, driven by new technologies, globalization, and urbanization.
- Industrialization of the food chain.
- The importance of these new sectors as income sources for the poor—farmer-owners as well as laborers.
- An important role for organizations other than state organizations—particularly private organizations, but also cooperatives and civil society organizations.

Table 1.1	World Value of Nontraditional Agricultural Exports, 1992 and 2001[a]		
US$ millions			
Exporters	**1992**	**2001**	**Growth (%)**
Developing countries	4,412	8,606	95
Developed countries	4,783	6,902	44

Source: FAO 2004.
a. Excludes citrus and bananas.

- The need to compete in rapidly evolving international markets and the consequent importance of innovation as a source of competitive advantage.
- The importance of upgrading and innovating, not only in high-technology sectors but also in sectors such as agriculture, which are considered more traditional and low-tech.
- The need to tailor innovation capacities to extremely heterogeneous and volatile conditions.

New agriculture is also an area where developing countries are competing successfully with developed countries. Table 1.1 shows that between 1992 and 2001 the export growth from developing countries was more than double the growth from the developed countries.

This study makes use of eight case studies from four countries—Bangladesh, India, Ghana, and Colombia—spanning the three main regions of the developing world—Asia, Africa, and Latin America (table 1.2; also see annex B). Four case studies (one per country) focus on truly new or nontraditional activities. The other four concentrate on more traditional sectors that are experiencing rapid transformation. The combination of traditional and nontraditional subsectors makes it possible to evaluate the suitability of the innovation systems concept across a wide range of conditions.

Table 1.2	Case Studies by Country and Subsector	
Case study country	**Traditional subsector in rapid transformation**	**Nontraditional subsector**
Bangladesh	Food processing	Shrimp
India	Medicinal plants	Vanilla
Ghana	Cassava processing	Pineapple
Colombia	Cassava processing	Cut flowers

Source: Authors.

ORGANIZATION OF THIS STUDY

The innovation systems concept is discussed more fully in chapter 2, especially with regard to its potential value for agricultural development interventions. It is also compared with earlier experience with the NARS and AKIS approaches. The discussion in the remainder of the chapter uses the innovation systems concept to develop an analytical framework to explore the nature of agricultural innovation and innovation capacity.

Chapter 3 describes the methodology for the study, further discusses the rationale for selecting each case study, and summarizes results of each study. The analysis of the case studies goes beyond understanding what stimulated innovation. It also identifies gaps in the innovation system by which interventions could improve the capacity for innovation. In chapter 4, a comparative analysis of the eight studies highlights differences in the evolution of the eight cases and identifies potential sources of these differences. The main findings from the case studies are used in chapter 5 to derive lessons on what drives innovation and the generic interventions that promote the capacity to innovate.

The comparative analysis of the case studies is used to develop an intervention framework (chapter 6). Based on the case studies, a typology of agricultural innovation environments is developed as a starting point for guiding the assessment of innovation capacity in different countries and sectors and for identifying the kinds of support that each might require. The intervention framework also makes use of diagnostic insights from the case studies to develop principles for intervention and for the sequencing of interventions. It gives examples of interventions that are tailored to the needs of each innovation environment. These interventions are designed to help strengthen innovation capacity and help arrangements evolve toward a dynamic, responsive, and sustainable system.

Chapter 7 recapitulates the main conclusions from the case studies, revisits the utility of the analytical framework for understanding agricultural innovation, and also revisits the value of the intervention framework for identifying activities in support of agricultural innovation. It concludes with a brief discussion of the implications for future investments by the World Bank.

CHAPTER TWO

The Innovation Systems Concept: A Framework for Analysis

cience and technology are critical to the development and economic growth strategies of both developed and developing countries. Scientific and technological knowledge and information add value to existing resources, skills, knowledge, and processes, leading to novel products, processes, and strategies. These innovations are the changes that lead to improvements in economic and social conditions and environmental sustainability. Innovation is therefore central to development.

The last 40 years have witnessed substantial debate over the best way for science and technology to foster innovation. At the risk of oversimplifying a complex reality, two distinct views may be outlined:

- *The first and earlier view* is that scientific research is the main driver of innovation, creating new knowledge and technology that can be transferred and adapted to different situations. *This view is usually described as the "linear" or "transfer of technology" model.*
- *The second view,* while not denying the importance of research and technology transfer, recognizes innovation as an interactive process. Innovation involves the interaction of individuals and organizations possessing different types of knowledge within a particular social, political, policy, economic, and institutional context. *This second view, increasingly discussed in terms of the "innovation system" concept, is the subject of this paper.*

These two perspectives emphasize different public policies and interventions to support innovation. The linear perspective concentrates on scientific research and the resources required for supporting and guiding (usually) public research and training organizations. The perspective of the innovation systems concept recognizes the importance of these activities but gives more attention to (1) the interaction between research and related economic activity, (2) the attitudes and practices that promote interaction and the learning that accompanies it, and (3) the creation of an enabling environment that encourages interaction and helps to put knowledge into socially and economically productive use. Critical differences in the perspectives are illustrated in box 2.1.

Following a brief discussion of the origins of the innovation systems concept, the next sections examine the analytical insights it provides, particularly in comparison with two other well-known frameworks for guiding capacity development and promoting innovation in the agricultural sector: the NARS and AKIS concepts (introduced briefly in chapter 1).

ORIGINS OF THE INNOVATION SYSTEMS CONCEPT

The innovation systems concept emerged through policy debates in developed countries in the 1970s and 1980s. These debates centered on the nature of industrial production in the developed world and the analytical frameworks required to explain patterns of industrial growth. At the time, industrial production was becoming more knowledge intensive as investments in intangibles such as research and development, software, design, engineering, training, marketing, and management came to play a greater role in the production of goods and services and in organizational competitiveness. Such investments often created tacit rather than codified knowledge. Unlike codified knowledge, which is explicit and recorded, tacit knowledge is difficult to articulate or write down; it is often embedded in skills, beliefs, or ways of doing things. Mastering tacit knowledge requires a conscious effort at learning by doing, by using, and by interacting (Mytelka 1987, 1999).

Gradually the knowledge intensity of production has extended beyond the high-tech sectors to reshape a broad spectrum of traditional industries—shrimp and salmon fisheries in the Philippines, Norway, and Chile (box 2.2); forestry and flower enterprises in Kenya, the Netherlands, and Colombia; and furniture, textile, and garment production in Indonesia, Italy, and Taiwan. Firms compete less on the basis of price and more on the basis of their ability to design novel products or improve the quality management of their production. Firms that anticipate or quickly adapt to changing consumer demand or changing production conditions are better placed to navigate between increasingly dynamic markets for consumer goods on the one hand and rapidly changing markets for raw materials and business-to-business services on the other.

According to Arnold and Bell (2001), the linear model of innovation mirrored the belief that "basic science leads to applied science, which causes innovation and wealth." The policy implications of this "science push" model were simple: "If you want more economic development, you fund more science." As more attention was given to the role of market forces in innovation, a corresponding (and equally linear) "market pull" model of innovation was developed (see box figure).

The linear model (which resembles an ivory tower on its side) captures the stereotypical image of research institutions laboring in isolation. In contrast, Arnold and Bell's depiction of a national innovation system shows the multiplicity of "actors and activities in the economy which are necessary for industrial and commercial innovation to take place and to lead to economic development" (p. 291). The central insight is that innovation depends as much on the performance of linkages between actors as on the performance of individuals. The implication, according to Arnold and Bell, is that "certain system characteristics—such as stronger links between actors—are likely to improve performance" (p. 293).

The set of potentially important actors in an innovation system differs from the string of suppliers and clients arranged along a classic value chain or the set of organizations involved in public sector research. There is no assumption that an innovation process starts with research or that knowledge feeds directly or automatically into new practices, processes, or products. Instead, the knowledge and information flows at the heart of an innovation system are multidirectional. They open opportunities for developing feedback loops that enhance competence building, learning, and adaptation. All too often, the right kinds of actors are absent, or they do not interact in ways that support the innovation process. The innovation systems concept helps to reveal why these interactions might not be present and what might be done to remedy this problem.

Linear Models

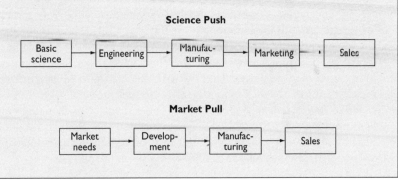

Science Push

Basic science → Engineering → Manufacturing → Marketing → Sales

Market Pull

Market needs → Development → Manufacturing → Sales

National Innovation System Model

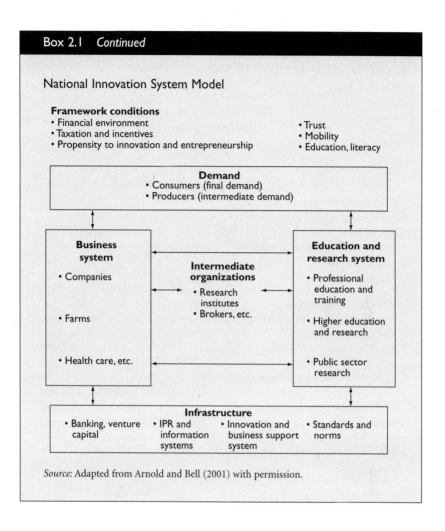

Framework conditions
- Financial environment
- Taxation and incentives
- Propensity to innovation and entrepreneurship
- Trust
- Mobility
- Education, literacy

Demand
- Consumers (final demand)
- Producers (intermediate demand)

Business system
- Companies
- Farms
- Health care, etc.

Intermediate organizations
- Research institutes
- Brokers, etc.

Education and research system
- Professional education and training
- Higher education and research
- Public sector research

Infrastructure
- Banking, venture capital
- IPR and information systems
- Innovation and business support system
- Standards and norms

Source: Adapted from Arnold and Bell (2001) with permission.

As traditional barriers to trade and investment have been dismantled, innovation-based competition has diffused around the globe. Local firms everywhere feel pressure to engage in continuous innovation, and they are challenging governments to develop policies to stimulate and support an innovation process.

Conventional economic models, which view innovation as a linear process driven by the supply of research and development (R&D), cannot fully explain these industry trends or offer much guidance for policy makers. Alternative explanations of the innovation process have emerged from the evolutionary economics tradition and other traditions (box 2.3). Several investigators observed that the more successful economies possessed what they described as an effective "national system of innovation" (Freeman 1987; Lundvall 1992). These

Exports of Chilean salmon rose from less than US$50 million in 1989 to US$1.7 billion in 2005. Salmon now accounts for close to 5 percent of Chile's exports. Chile's share of world salmon production moved from 2 percent in 1987 to nearly 25 percent by the end of the 1990s. The country's comparative advantage in salmon production derived not only from its natural resources—pure waters and good ecological conditions—but from the alertness of local entrepreneurs and the readiness of public and public-private agencies to help the industry take off.

In the early years—the late 1970s and early 1980s—small firms were concerned mainly with overcoming their highly imperfect understanding of the technological, organizational, and ecological/environmental conditions for salmon production. Trial and error and firm-specific learning were the major characteristics of firms' behavior during those years. Government played a crucial catalytic role in the design of plants and in other forms of knowledge generation and diffusion.

In the ensuing period of rapid growth, a public-private system grew up around salmon farming in Chile. New firms entered the market, capacity expanded, and process improvements were embodied in new machinery and equipment—brought almost entirely from abroad, however. The public sector contributed by building roads, modernizing docks and shipping facilities, and inducing firms—through regulatory agencies—to adopt international quality norms and standards. At present, the industry is much more capital intensive. Firms are larger and technologically more complex. The more dynamic ones are proceeding into products with a higher domestic value added, competing globally by selling under proprietary trademarks to large international retailers.

The future of the industry is not assured, however. Chile's salmon-farming sector has failed to develop a strong capacity to generate and export knowledge and technology. Nor has it induced the expansion of the capital goods industry catering to salmon farming. Once again—as in the early years of salmon farming—government must play a catalytic role if the industry is to move to the next knowledge-intensive stage of development. One alternative is for the government to coordinate collective action among salmon-farming firms, public-private knowledge-generation institutions, and financing agencies, with an eye to overcoming market failures in the generation and dissemination of knowledge.

Source: Katz 2006.

Box 2.3 Theoretical Underpinnings of Innovation Systems

Various streams of economics thinking are helpful in understanding how drivers of growth are changing and the resulting implications for managing innovation.

- *New growth theory* stresses the importance of increasing returns to knowledge accumulation, based on investment in new technologies and human capital.
- *Evolutionary and industrial economics* demonstrates that this accumulation is a learning process that involves interactions between the different stages of research and innovation and is shaped by the interplay of market and nonmarket organizations (such as networks and social norms or regulations).
- *Institutional economics* stresses the importance of organizational innovation within firms and governments in the design and coordination of institutions and procedures involved in handling more complex interdependencies, as growth leads to the increasing specialization of tasks and productive tools.
- *Sociology of innovation* stresses the role of "trust" in avoiding the escalating transaction costs that result from increased specialization and the role of institutional and cultural variety in boosting creativity.

Source: OECD 2001, Guinet 2004.

systems developed in an institutional (often network-based) setting, which fostered interaction and learning among scientific and entrepreneurial actors in the public and private sector in response to changing economic and technical conditions. The continuous process of innovation that emerged from this setting was viewed as central to the economic success of countries such as Japan in the1980s.

Over time, the innovation systems concept has gained wide support among the member countries of the Organisation for Economic Co-operation and Development (OECD). More recently the concept has been applied in the European Union (EU)[3] and in a number of developing countries as a framework for policy analysis (OECD 1997; Wong 1999; Cassiolato, Lastres, and Maciel 2003). Although the innovation systems concept is relatively new to agricultural policy makers and agricultural research managers in developing countries, it is increasingly suggested as a way of revisiting the question of how to strengthen agricultural innovation capacity (Hall et al. 2001; Clark et al. 2003; Hall 2005).

INNOVATION VERSUS INVENTION

To understand the relationship between science and technology and economic change, it is important to understand that innovation is not synonymous with invention. As mentioned in chapter 1, invention culminates in the supply (creation) of knowledge, but innovation encompasses the factors affecting demand for and use of knowledge in novel and useful ways. The notion of *novelty* is fundamental to invention, but the notion of the *process of creating local change, new to the user,* is fundamental to innovation—specifically, the process by which organizations "master and implement the design and production of goods and services that are new to them irrespective of whether they are new to their competitors, their country, or the world" (Mytelka 2000, p. 18). Goel et al. (2004) summarize the relationship between invention and innovation more succinctly: "Knowledge is transformed into goods and services through a country's national innovation system" (p. 14).

Distinguishing characteristics of innovations and the innovation process include the following:

- Innovations are new creations of social and economic significance. They may be brand new, but they are more often new combinations of existing elements.
- Innovation can comprise radical improvements, but it usually consists of many small improvements and a continuous process of upgrading.
- These improvements may be of a technical, managerial, institutional (that is, the way things are routinely done), or policy nature.
- Very often innovations involve a combination of technical, institutional, and other sorts of changes.
- Innovation can be triggered in many ways. Bottlenecks in production within a firm, changes in available technology, competitive conditions, international trade rules, domestic regulations, or environmental health concerns may all trigger innovation processes (Rosenberg 1976; Dosi et al. 1988).

KEY INSIGHTS FROM THE INNOVATION SYSTEMS CONCEPT FOR DIAGNOSTIC AND INTERVENTION FRAMEWORKS

An innovation system can be defined as a network of organizations focused on bringing new products, new processes, and new forms of organization into social and economic use, together with the institutions and policies that affect their behavior and performance. The following paragraphs summarize 11 analytical insights on the innovation systems concept. These insights are used later in this paper to develop a framework for using the innovation systems concept to diagnose the strengths and weaknesses of existing innovation capacity as well as to guide investments and interventions to strengthen this capacity.

ENHANCING AGRICULTURAL INNOVATION

1. A focus on innovation rather than production. In contrast to most economic frameworks, which focus on production or output, the focus here is on *innovation.* Innovation is understood to be neither research nor science and technology, but rather the application of knowledge (of all types) in the production of goods and services to achieve desired social or economic outcomes. So, for example, the development of a new packaging material by a research organization or a company is an invention. In contrast, a company packaging its product in a new way using new or existing information is an innovation.

2. Interaction and learning. Innovation is an interactive process through which knowledge acquisition and learning take place. This process often requires quite extensive linkages with different knowledge sources. These sources may be scientific and technical, but equally they can be a source of other forms of knowledge, both tacit and codified. Patterns of interaction between different knowledge sources form a central component of an organization's or sector's capacity to innovate. Ideas like the creation of science parks are one response to the need to strengthen the intensity of interaction to promote the process of innovation.

3. Linkages for accessing knowledge and learning. The relationships that sustain the acquisition of knowledge and permit interactive learning are critical and can take many forms. They can be partnerships, for example, in which two or more organizations pool knowledge and resources and jointly develop a product, or they can be commercial transactions, in which an organization purchases technologies (in which knowledge is embedded) or knowledge services from another organization, in which case the relationship is defined by a contract or license. Linkages may also take the form of networks, which provide an organization with market and other early-warning intelligence on changing consumer preferences or technology. Networks also embody the "know who" of knowledge sources, which can be tapped as the need arises. These linkages and the relationships that govern them concern knowledge flows. They must not be confused with the linkages and relationships that govern the movement of commodities through value chains, although many of the same actors may be involved.

4. New actors, new roles. In the linear model of innovation, especially with respect to developing country agriculture, public research organizations are the prime movers. Following this model, scientists have undertaken research, their extension services have transferred technology, and these roles have remained compartmentalized and relatively static, even as the external environment has changed (for instance, as the private sector began to participate more). The innovation systems concept recognizes that (1) there is an important role for a broad spectrum of actors outside government (box 2.4); (2) the actors' relative importance changes during the innovation process; (3) as circumstances change and actors learn, roles can evolve; and (4) actors can play multiple roles (for example, at various times they can be sources of knowledge, seekers of knowledge, and coordinators of links between others [Hall 2006; Mytelka 2004a, 2004b]).

5. Attitudes and practices that determine the propensity to innovate. The
common attitudes, routines, practices, rules, or laws that regulate the relationships and interactions between individuals and groups largely determine the
propensity of actors and organizations to innovate (Edquist 1997). Some
organizations have a tradition of interacting with other organizations; others
tend to work in isolation. Some have a tradition of sharing information with
collaborators and competitors, of learning and upgrading, whereas others are
more conservative in this respect. Some resist risk-taking; others do not. Table
2.1 gives examples of commonly encountered attitudes and practices that affect
the processes important to innovation.

6. Interaction of behavioral patterns and innovation triggers. Attitudes and
practices also determine how organizations respond to innovation triggers such
as changing policies, markets, and technology. Because such attitudes vary across
organizations and across countries and regions, actors in different sectors or
countries may not respond in the same ways to the same set of innovation triggers. Interventions that seek to develop the capacity for innovation must give

Table 2.1 Attitudes and Practices Affecting Key Innovation Processes and Relationships

Process	Restrictive attitudes and practices	Supportive attitudes and practices
Interaction, knowledge flows, learning	- Mistrust of other organizations - Closed to others' ideas - Secretiveness - Lack of confidence - Professional hierarchies between organizations and disciples - Internal hierarchies - Top-down cultures and approaches - Covering up of failures - Limited scope and intensity of interaction in sector networks	- Trust - Openness - Transparency - Confidence - Mutual respect - Flat management structure - Reflection and learning from successes and failures - Proactive networking
Inclusiveness of poor stakeholders and the demand side	- Hierarchies - Top-down cultures and approaches	- Consultative and participatory attitudes
Risk-taking and investment	- Conservative	- Confidence - Professional incentives

Source: Authors.

particular attention to ingrained attitudes and practices and the way these are likely to interact with and skew the outcome of interventions (Engel and Salomon 1997).

7. The role of policies. Policy support of innovation is not the outcome of a single policy but of a set of policies that work together to shape innovative behavior. In evaluating the effectiveness of policies on innovative performance, investigators must therefore be sensitive to a wide range of policies that affect innovation and seek ways of coordinating them. Moreover, policies interact with attitudes and practices, and thus, effective policies must take account of existing behavioral patterns (Mytelka 2000). For example, the introduction of more participatory approaches to research is often ineffective unless scientists' attitudes (and incentives) are changed. Similarly, food safety regulations might be rendered ineffective if the agencies charged with enforcing them have a tradition of rent-seeking behavior. Policies to promote innovation must be attuned to specific contexts.

8. Inclusion of stakeholders and the demand side. The innovation systems concept recognizes the importance of the inclusion of stakeholders and the development of behavioral patterns that make organizations and policies sensitive to stakeholders' agendas or demands (Engel 1997). Stakeholders' demands are important signals that can shape the focus and direction of innovation processes. They are not articulated by the market alone but can be expressed through a number of other channels, such as collaborative relationships between users and producers of knowledge, or mutual participation in organizational governance (for example, board membership). For an example, see box 2.5.

9. *Learning and capacity building.* The attitudes and practices critical to innovation are themselves learned behaviors that shape approaches and arrangements and are continuously changing in both incremental and radical ways. These changes include institutional innovations that emerge through scientists' experimentation and learning, such as farmer field schools or participatory plant breeding. Alternatively a company may start using research to gain an edge over its competitors. Another example would be organizational learning to discover that partnering is a key strategy for responding rapidly to emerging market opportunities. The new ways of working that result from learning enhance the ability of organizations and sectors to access and use knowledge more effectively and therefore to innovate. For this reason, the capability to learn to work in new ways and to incrementally build new competencies is an important part of innovation capacity at the organization and sector or systems level.

10. *Change to cope with change.* The classic response of more successful innovation systems, when they are faced with external shocks, is to reconfigure linkages or networks of partners (Mytelka and Farinelli 2003). A new pest problem may require new alliances between scientific disciplines; a new technology, such as biotechnology, could require partnerships between the public and private sector; or changing trade rules and competitive pressure in international markets could require new alliances between local companies and between those companies and research organizations. It is impossible to be prescriptive about the types of networks, linkages, and partnerships that, for example, agricultural research organizations will need in the future, because the nature of future shocks and triggers is unknown and to a large extent unknowable. One way of dealing with this uncertainty, however, is to develop attitudes that encourage dynamic and rapid responses to changing circumstances—by building self-confidence and trust, fostering preparedness for change, and stimulating creativity.

11. *Ability to cope with "sticky" information.* A number of key insights discussed above emphasize that innovation can be based on different kinds of knowledge possessed by different actors: local, context-specific knowledge (which farmers and other users of technology typically possess) and generic knowledge (which scientists and other producers of technology typically possess). In an ideal innovation system, a two-way flow of information exists between these sources of knowledge, but in reality this flow is often constrained

Box 2.5 Including Stakeholders' Demands in the Agricultural Innovation System: Mexico's Produce Foundations

In 1996, Mexico established the Fundaciones Produce (Produce Foundations) in all of its 32 states to entrust producers with the management of operating funds previously allocated to the national agricultural research organization (INIFAP). Initially INIFAP had a guaranteed share of the resources. This guarantee was removed in 1998, and in subsequent years the share of other providers of research services, such as universities and nonagricultural research institutes, increased.

By directly involving producers in decisions on research and innovation, the foundations have helped address the long-felt need to improve links between activities in the research system and farmers' requirements for technology and knowledge. Researchers have learned to negotiate with farmers and to combine their perceptions of scientific opportunities with farmers' urgent technological needs.

The foundations actively developed innovation programs for key sectors and quickly established a role for themselves as respected innovation intermediaries in Mexican agriculture. They took four important steps to prepare for this role. First, they realized that although each foundation was based on the same principles, it would probably have a lot to learn from the others. Second, the foundations organized themselves as a national coordinating agency (COFUPRO) to be in a better position to influence decision making at the national level. Third, they engaged in a strategic partnership with the National Council on Science and Technology (CONACYT) to increase their financial leverage. Finally, they trained themselves in diagnostic, research planning, and research management approaches and developed a national catalogue of research needs.

The foundations have helped in the transformation of the research system, created communication channels between the government and farmers, and started to manage other agricultural development projects. They have quickly become a key player in Mexico's agricultural sector.

Source: Ekboir et al. forthcoming.

because information is embodied in different actors who are not networked or coordinated. In these circumstances, information does not flow easily; it is "sticky." A central challenge in designing innovation systems is to overcome this asymmetry—in other words, to discover how to bring those possessing locally specific knowledge (farmers or local entrepreneurs) closer to those possessing generic knowledge (researchers or actors with access to large-scale product development, market placement, or financing technologies). Ways of dealing with this asymmetry include the following:

- *Encouraging user innovation.* For example, as the capacity of the private sector grows, the private sector will undertake a greater proportion of innovation, because it possesses the fundamental advantage of knowing the market.
- *Developing innovation platforms for learning, sharing, communicating, and innovating.* The structure of public research systems must adapt to permit a more open, thorough, and multifaceted dialogue with other key actors identified in the innovation system analysis.
- *Investing in public research and advisory systems.* Such investment must be based on careful identification of knowledge demands and joint strategic planning with the multiple stakeholders of the system.

INNOVATION SYSTEMS AND VALUE CHAINS

Innovation systems and value chains often have many shared partners, and although they respond to different organizational principles, they are highly complementary and overlapping. (A value chain may be defined as the set of interconnected, value-creating activities undertaken by an enterprise or group of enterprises to develop, produce, deliver, and maintain a product or service.) From a value chain perspective, the key challenge is to link supply and demand in the most effective way, and information sharing is very important for enabling these producer-consumer linkages. Organizations that help to link producers, transporters, and distributors to consumer markets are vital if value chains are to function effectively. When participants in a value chain pass along information on demand characteristics, for example, or on standards and regulations affecting the market (such as sanitary and phytosanitary standards), at the same time they are providing important information to shape the direction of the innovation process. If, in addition to a well-functioning value chain, an effective innovation capacity exists, this market information will be combined with new and existing knowledge on technological opportunities and information, such as farming techniques, postharvest processes, and marketing to innovate in response to these market signals. One of the innovation challenges with respect to sustainable agriculture is to expand opportunities and means for resource-poor farmers to become actors and stakeholders in these innovation systems (boxes 2.6 and 2.7).

In summary, a value chain brings partners together in their desire to integrate production, marketing, and consumption issues in the most profitable way, both in the long run and in the short run. For example, value chain partners may need to make organizational and technological changes, or they may need to agree on pricing practices or quality control systems. The innovation system perspective brings actors together in their desire to introduce or create novelty or innovation in the value chain, allowing it to respond in a dynamic way to an array of market, policy, and other signals. The innovation systems perspective provides a way of planning how to create and apply new knowledge

Agriculture in western China is characterized by deep rural poverty linked to traditional production systems. World Bank support is focusing on assisting the national plan to restructure and modernize the sector. An especially innovative part of this effort is the development and testing of tripartite joint ventures between agribusinesses, small-scale farmers, and research providers to enhance knowledge-based value addition in agricultural production, especially farmers' share of the value added. The focus on partnerships grew out of an assessment of rural communities and their links with public and private stakeholders, which revealed the following:

- Increasingly complex and nonlinear linkages from research to product, with networks for public and private partners engaged in innovation, development, production, and marketing.
- Consumer demand–driven research agendas, including the integration of agricultural production and emerging environmental sustainability agendas (such as integrated pest management and "green" food).
- A changing public sector role, away from productive activities and toward the setting and enforcing of regulatory frameworks and quality standards.

Partners in these joint ventures (researcher/research institution, company, and farmer/farmer association) enter into a risk- and benefit-sharing arrangement in the form of contracts, joint shareholding, or revenue sharing, which guarantees that benefits are not captured by one partner alone. Farmer organizations have legal support for negotiating contracts. This institutional arrangement seeks to ensure that new products and technologies propagated, developed, or under development respond to market demand, are supported by research to stay competitive, and involve farmer organizations as business partners to ensure fair benefit sharing.

Source: Adapted from World Bank 2006a.

required for the development, adaptation, and future profitability of the value chain.

COMPARISON OF NARS, AKIS, AND AGRICULTURAL INNOVATION SYSTEMS

What does the innovation systems concept bring to the task of promoting change that other frameworks have missed? It is instructive to compare it with two

Box 2.7 Community-Driven Development and Agricultural Innovation Systems

The World Bank channels approximately US$2 billion in annual lending using the community-driven development (CDD) approach, which empowers local communities to take ownership of their development process. CDD is not a model for development but rather an approach that promotes four general principles:

1. Make investments responsive to informed demand and facilitate community access to information.
2. Build participatory mechanisms for community control and stakeholder involvement, with special consideration for social and gender inclusion.
3. Invest in building the capacity of community-based organizations.
4. Establish enabling institutional and policy frameworks, including simple, clear rules and strong incentives supported by monitoring and evaluation.

For much of the 1990s, the Bank's CDD investments focused on developing public services and building social capital at the local level. As communities have gained access to basic services that they once lacked, their needs have changed. The focus now is to transform the social capital from earlier efforts into economic capital to raise the productivity and income of communities. In rural areas, this emphasis is reflected in an increase in the number of agricultural investments that have used CDD, which has averaged about 40 percent of agricultural projects over the past three years.

The innovation systems framework clearly complements the CDD approach: local communities and their institutions (built and strengthened through CDD) can become partners in the innovation process by seeking alliances with producer organizations and research organizations. The capital accumulated within rural communities through CDD is an asset that communities can use to scale up production and become an attractive partner for the agribusiness sector, and it can also give communities a stronger voice in negotiating the terms of engagement with the private sector. Moving forward, the vision for CDD is to foster sustainable local economies that participate fully in the local, regional, national, and global innovation systems.

Source: World Bank 2002.

major frameworks for planning capacity development: NARS and AKIS. The main characteristics of these two frameworks are described in the following sections, followed by a discussion of their major similarities and differences (summarized in table 2.2).

Table 2.2 Defining Features of the NARS and AKIS Frameworks in Relation to Agricultural Innovation Systems

Defining feature	NARS	AKIS[a]	Agricultural innovation system
Purpose	Planning capacity for agricultural research, technology development, and technology transfer	Strengthening communication and knowledge delivery services to people in the rural sector	Strengthening the capacity to innovate throughout the agricultural production and marketing system
Actors	National agricultural research organizations, agricultural universities or faculties of agriculture, extension services, and farmers	National agricultural research organizations, agricultural universities or faculties of agriculture, extension services, farmers, NGOs, and entrepreneurs in rural areas	Potentially all actors in the public and private sectors involved in the creation, diffusion, adaptation, and use of all types of knowledge relevant to agricultural production and marketing
Outcome	Technology invention and technology transfer	Technology adoption and innovation in agricultural production	Combinations of technical and institutional innovations throughout the production, marketing, policy research, and enterprise domains
Organizing principle	Using science to create inventions	Accessing agricultural knowledge	Finding new uses of knowledge for social and economic change
Mechanism for innovation	Transfer of technology	Interactive learning	Interactive learning
Degree of market integration	None	Low	High
Role of policy	Resource allocation, priority setting	Enabling framework	Integrated component and enabling framework
Nature of capacity strengthening	Infrastructure and human resource development	Strengthening of communication between actors in rural areas	Strengthening of interactions between actors; institutional development and change to support interaction, learning, and innovation; creating an enabling environment

Source: FAO and World Bank 2000; ISNAR 1992; authors.
a. As defined by FAO and World Bank 2000.

National Agricultural Research Systems

A NARS comprises all of the entities within a country that are responsible for organizing, coordinating, or executing research that contributes explicitly to the development of its agriculture and the maintenance of its natural resource base (ISNAR 1992). The NARS framework has been the mainstay of agricultural development planning for the past 40 years or so. The underlying idea is classically linear: agricultural research, through technology transfer, leads to technology adoption and growth in productivity. The capacity to achieve this goal lies within the agricultural research, training, and extension organizations of the public sector. Capacity is developed by investing in scientific infrastructure, equipping human resources with up-to-date skills, setting research priorities, and providing the operational funds to implement those priorities. This model proved very effective in areas where technological solutions with wide potential applicability were required (for example, to overcome the food shortages in South Asia in the 1970s). The emphasis on setting priorities by agricultural commodity implies that small and nascent activities tend to be neglected until they have reached significant economic importance. The NARS framework highlights the research base that leads to improved production technology, although in practice, the adoption of these research results in farmers' fields is often encouraged by separate output and input (especially fertilizer) pricing policies.

Strengths. The NARS framework has been effective in creating agricultural science capacity and in making improved varieties of major food staples available, particularly in Asia, where its use has transformed food production.

Limitations. Research is not explicitly linked to technology users and other actors in the sector. As a result, NARS priorities are slow to reflect clients' needs and changing circumstances in the sector. The NARS framework is poorly suited for responding to rapidly changing market conditions and for providing technologies for producers to supply emerging, high-value niche markets. By emphasizing the development of the capacity of the research system, the NARS framework tends to limit attention to other factors that enable new technologies to be used (although some efforts have been made to overcome this limitation; see box 2.8).

Agricultural Knowledge and Information Systems

Agricultural knowledge and information systems link people and organizations to promote mutual learning and to generate, share, and use agriculture-related technology, knowledge, and information. An AKIS integrates farmers, agricultural educators, researchers, and extension staff to harness knowledge and information from various sources for improved livelihoods. Farmers are at the heart of the knowledge triangle formed by education, research, and extension (FAO and World Bank 2000).

The AKIS framework has its origins in the analysis of agricultural extension arrangements. It has a strong focus on how information and ideas are com-

Comparisons of linear and networked models of innovation inevitably focus on their critical differences, but in reality many research systems fall somewhere on the spectrum between these two extremes. Over the years, some research systems have sought to break away from the insularity of the linear model by experimenting with participatory, grassroots, and multistakeholder approaches. For example, on-farm research and rapid rural appraisal methods developed in the late 1970s and 1980s explicitly sought to involve scientists in drawing on farmers' knowledge and enabling farmers to participate fully in planning, executing, and evaluating research. More recent efforts include the following:

- *Farmer, private sector, and other stakeholder participation on research governing boards and advisory panels,* to attain real influence over research decisions and priorities. Participation of women farmers is particularly important, given their crucial role in rural production systems, the special constraints under which they operate (for example, time constraints), and their range of activities and enterprises, including marketing, agro-processing, and food storage.
- *Decentralized research,* to bring scientists closer to clients and better focus research on local problems and opportunities.
- *Decentralized extension services* accountable to local user groups, to facilitate clients' "purchase" of research services and products that respond to their needs. Matching grant programs for farmer and community groups allow them to test and disseminate new technologies.
- *Competitive funding,* to promote demand-driven research by involving key stakeholders, especially users, in setting priorities, formulating projects, and screening proposals.

Although these efforts have not always been successful within the bounds of traditional research systems, they represent a growing spectrum of initiatives to engage farmers and others more fully in the research process. The result is that many agricultural research systems have already adopted characteristics of innovation systems. However, in all of these efforts the centrality of research as the driver of innovation is still maintained.

municated between the various actors in rural areas and how this knowledge can be harnessed for rural livelihoods. AKIS recognizes learning and innovation as an interactive process. The AKIS framework has been promoted strongly by the United Nation's Food and Agriculture Organization (FAO) and tackles many of the shortcomings of conventional agricultural research and extension systems, particularly their limited opportunities for interaction between the users and producers of knowledge.

Strengths. The AKIS concept recognizes that multiple sources of knowledge contribute to agricultural innovation and gives attention to developing channels of communication between them. The emphasis on innovation as a social process of learning broadens the scope of agricultural research and extension to include developing local capacities. The addition of educators to the framework is notable. The AKIS framework clearly recognizes that education improves farmers' ability to engage in innovation processes.

Limitations. The focus is restricted to actors and processes in the rural environment, and the framework pays limited attention to the role of markets (especially input and output markets), the private sector, the enabling policy environment, and other disciplines/sectors. The AKIS framework recognizes the importance of transferring information from farmers to research systems but tends to suggest that most technologies will be transferred from researchers down to farmers.

Agricultural Innovation Systems

The innovation systems concept values the capacities and processes emphasized in the NARS and AKIS frameworks, including channels that give farmers access to information, and well-resourced and up-to-date scientific research and training organizations. The innovation systems concept goes further in recognizing a broader range of actors and disciplines/sectors involved in innovation, particularly the private sector in its many guises along the value chain. Innovation systems analysis recognizes that creating an enabling environment to support the use of knowledge is as important as making that knowledge available through research and dissemination mechanisms.

In the same way, an innovation system encompasses a wider set of activities that are likely to support innovation by including such processes as the creative adaptation and financing of innovation. Like AKIS, the innovation systems concept places greater emphasis on the interaction between actors, but the innovation systems concept encompasses a wider set of relationships that can potentially foster innovation. Because the innovation systems concept includes this broader set of relationships between actors and contexts, it potentially offers a framework for embedding innovation capacities in the rapidly changing market, technological, social, and political environment of contemporary agriculture.

Strengths. The innovation systems concept, which has been tested widely in the industrial sector, offers a holistic way of strengthening the capacity to create, diffuse, and use knowledge. Aside from knowledge and skills, capacity development includes the attitudes and practices that influence the way organizations deal with knowledge, learning, and innovation and the patterns of relationships and interactions that exist between different organizations. The concept strongly links innovation and investment needs.

Limitations. The innovation systems concept remains largely untested in the agricultural sector. It is difficult to diagnose the interactions and institutional dimensions of innovation capacity from analysis of published data sources, as these are not routinely tracked in industry and national statistics. Less emphasis is placed on education.

TOWARD PRACTICAL APPLICATIONS OF THE INNOVATION SYSTEMS CONCEPT

This chapter has described the origins and comparative strengths and weaknesses of the innovation systems concept to lay the groundwork for addressing the practical concerns that lie at the heart of this paper. The next chapter discusses how the eight case studies were organized in Asia, Africa, and Latin America to evaluate the potential for applying the innovation systems concept in various agricultural settings throughout the developing world. The research methodology, the instruments developed to guide the collection of information, and criteria for selecting the case studies are described. A synopsis of each study is provided.

CHAPTER THREE

Research Methodology and Case Study Descriptions

RESEARCH METHODOLOGY

The starting point for the eight case studies undertaken in South Asia (India and Bangladesh), Sub-Saharan Africa (Ghana), and Latin America (Colombia) was to develop a conceptual framework that could guide the analysis of innovation systems in these settings. A background paper developed and reviewed prior to commissioning the studies (Hall, Mytelka, and Oyeyinka 2004) outlined the conceptual framework (described in the previous chapter) and methodological guidelines for the case studies, which are summarized in this chapter and provided in annex A.

The conceptual framework places great emphasis on understanding the nature of relationships between actors and the attitudes and practices that shape those relationships. Relationships promote interaction, and interaction promotes learning and innovation. Information on such qualitative processes usually is not available in databases[4] and was not available to the researchers who undertook the case studies. To assess these features of the innovation system, researchers relied on a checklist of issues to be investigated (box 3.1) and a number of tools to explore partnerships, attitudes, and practices. The tools included (1) an actor linkage matrix tool for mapping patterns of interaction; (2) a typology tool for differentiating among forms of relationships; (3) a typology of different forms of learning (a key innovation process) and the partnerships needed to sustain the learning; and (4) a typology of attitudes and practices that shape the key interaction patterns, the propensity to include poor stakeholders, and the willingness to take risks.

The following checklist was developed to guide diagnostic assessments for the case studies and the options for intervention discussed in the remainder of this paper. The checklist is designed to address a central idea from the innovation systems concept: partnerships and linkages are central to innovative performance and must be analyzed in their historical and contemporary context to understand their strengths and weaknesses.

The historical context explains why organizations do things the way they do—for example, why industry associations in some sectors are active only in political lobbying and not in technological upgrading for the sector. In other words, it gives an explanation of the origins and limitations of the attitudes and practices that determine the capacity of companies, countries, and sectors to innovate. The context includes policy, market, and trade conditions and the challenges and opportunities they present, as well as other contextual factors, such as the sociopolitical environment and the natural resource base. The extent to which attitudes and practices interact with the new demands also defines actors' ability to innovate in a responsive way. So, for example, if international patterns of competition demand that national companies interact and collaborate to develop new marketing strategies (an innovation), the attitudes and practices of companies with regard to such collaboration will determine their ability to innovate in response to the new demands within the sector.

A description of the changing context is therefore a key diagnostic element for revealing any divergence between organizations/other actors and their practices (on the one hand) and the changing demands imposed by the context (on the other). An exploration of these issues is the unique contribution of the innovation systems concept.

These ideas were used to develop the following checklist:

Actors, roles they play, and activities in which they are involved:
- Is a sufficiently diverse set of organizations from the public and private sector actively engaged in a sector?
- Is the range of actors appropriate to the nature of the sector, the stage of development of the market, and the institutional setting of the particular country?

Attitudes and practices of the main actors:
- What attitudes enable or restrict collaboration between organizations?
- What ineffective or conservative behavior can be identified?
- Do patterns of trust and reciprocity exist to serve as foundations for evolving and future collaboration across the innovation system?

continued

Box 3.1 *Continued*

- Does a culture of innovation exist? For example, is there a demand for research in the private sector? Is there an emphasis on capacity building for future eventualities? Or do organizations simply deal reactively with their present problems and opportunities? Is the use of collaborative arrangements for knowledge-based activities common? Is there an emphasis on both technological learning (mastering new technology) and institutional learning (accessing and using knowledge more effectively)?

Patterns of interaction:
- Are there networks and partnerships between private companies, farmer organizations, NGOs, and research and policy organizations?
- Are the concerns of the poor integrated in the activities of the innovation systems, and are there mechanisms to promote their agenda?
- Are sector-coordinating bodies present or absent? If present, are they effective?
- Are stakeholder bodies, such as farmer and industry associations, present or absent? If they are present, what is the scope of their knowledge-based activities (research, training, technology acquisition, market and technology forecasting)?

Enabling environment (policies and infrastructure):
- Are there science and technology policies to promote collaboration (such as competitive grant funds for partnerships), to scale up innovations (such as incubators or venture capital), or to encourage private research investments (such as matching grants)?
- Do fiscal policies promote research and development?
- Are farmer and other organizations involved in defining research and innovation challenges?
- Do legal frameworks exist to facilitate the application of new knowledge from within or outside the country?

A comparative analysis of the eight case studies (chapter 4) focused on how the innovation process differed across the cases. It identified specific factors that triggered, enabled, or prevented innovation and analyzed how they were linked with the factors described in the checklist. The comparative analysis also explored which types of interventions successfully enabled innovation.

CASE STUDY SELECTION

Part of the rationale for exploring the utility of the innovation systems concept is that old analytical frameworks, with their associated "traditional" systems for generating research and knowledge, cannot deal with the rapidly changing context for agriculture in many countries. As mentioned in chapter 1, these features include a more prominent role for the private sector; a more dynamic policy, market, technology, and environmental context; the emergence of niche sectors showing strong patterns of growth, such as horticulture, aquaculture, and food processing; stronger integration of the agricultural sector in international markets and consequent exposure to global trade rules; rapid urbanization and associated changing food preferences; increased processing of traditional commodities, often accompanied by a blurring of the distinction between agriculture and industry and the industrialization of the food chain; and, in response to these trends, the emergence of new opportunities—and new impediments—to use agricultural development as a means of reducing poverty and fostering sustainable development.

Four main criteria were used to select case studies that would capture elements of this dynamic agricultural context: (1) niche sectors that had shown strong patterns of growth; (2) sectors that were strongly integrated into global markets; (3) traditional sectors that are being transformed by the growth of activities further up the food chain and that can then highlight implications of the industrialization of the food chain; and (4) sectors that provide large employment opportunities to the poor. Table 3.1 lists the case studies in relation to the selection criteria.

INFORMATION COLLECTION

Researchers from the case study country or region were selected to conduct each case study. They received the conceptual framework document, the methodological guidelines, and a report structure. They also received training in the methodology and were visited during the research to provide assistance in using the methodology.

The researchers assembled secondary data, reports, and studies, and they also collected primary data through interviews of key informants from companies, farmers, research organization staff, industry bodies, farmer associations, public coordinating organizations (such as commodity boards), government ministries, and policy analysis institutes. This information was used to develop a description and a diagnostic assessment of the innovation system, which were presented in the case study report.

CASE STUDY DESCRIPTIONS

Shrimp in Bangladesh

The sector. Growth of the shrimp sector was set off in the 1970s mainly by individual export companies that competed on the basis of price and supplied

Table 3.1 Case Studies and Selection Criteria

Sector and country	Niche sector with history of strong growth	Export sector integrated in the global market	Traditional sector in agroindustrial transformation	Sectors with large employment potential
Shrimp, Bangladesh	X	X		X
Food processing, Bangladesh	X		X	X
Medicinal plants, India	X	X	X	X
Vanilla, India	X	X		
Pineapple, Ghana	X	X		
Cassava processing, Ghana	Emergent	Emergent	X	
Cassava processing, Colombia	Emergent	Emergent	X	
Cut flowers, Colombia	X	X		X

Source: Authors (integrated from various reports).

markets characterized by limited regulation. The global context has changed radically. The sector now must (1) comply with increasingly regulated markets, such as the U.S. Food and Drug Administration's Hazard Analysis Critical Control Point (HACCP) seafood regulation, (2) address the environmental protection and social equity considerations associated with shrimp production, (3) compete with cheaper producers, mainly in South America, and (4) build a reputation of quality by enforcing standards and certification.

Main actors. Entrepreneurs setting up shrimp processing and export companies have driven the industry's growth. Those companies operated and explored markets largely independently. Efforts to coordinate and regulate the sector have been undertaken by different actors (the Department of Fisheries, industry associations, and policy research and advocacy groups) but have been relatively unsuccessful. National and international research agencies are active in Bangladesh, although it is unclear how they have supported the shrimp sector. NGOs have provided technical support to poor shrimp farmers but have been inefficient in linking farmers with the market and the domestic policy process.

Interaction mechanisms and innovation. For historical and institutional reasons, the actors in the shrimp sector are highly fragmented. Local practices and social relations that restrict the sector's ability to respond to new challenges include (1) a highly individual business culture that lacks a collaborative tradition; (2) a reactive approach to problem solving through technical assistance financed by the government, international donors, or NGOs; and (3) the industry's lack of confidence in the research community. The social and political context also tends to reinforce relations between the government and large industrial firms in ways that exclude the poor and undermine their ability to innovate. Although relationships within the market chain are well developed, all other forms of interaction are very weak—within the industry (that is, among firms), between the industry and the research community, between the industry and the government, and between NGOs and the aforementioned actors.

Enabling environment. The government has supported the shrimp sector by developing infrastructure. Quality standards and environmental policies are in place, but the political and institutional context operating in Bangladesh has prevented the government from enforcing them. Compliance with these policies has been easier for the formal, large-scale industry than for informal, small-scale producers and has not always occurred through fair means. Poor compliance harms the country's competitive position in international markets because it undermines the national brand image.

Ways forward. The real challenge for the shrimp sector is to address the different challenges (market, social, environmental, quality) in an integrated manner and to build coherent, collaborative action across the sector. In the current sociopolitical context, it is questionable whether the government—and likewise, the main players in the export industry—can be sufficiently neutral to coordinate the sector efficiently and foster an integrated approach. Progress requires the creation of an efficient sector-coordinating body with members drawn from the public and private sector, including the national and international research community, NGOs and other producer representatives, and representatives from major importing countries. Some of the key functions might include an improved understanding of market and quality requirements, as well as coordinated action to meet specific industry and export requirements and to help producers link with markets and reap some of the value added provided by the sector. Collaboration with foreign shrimp-processing companies could expose the local industry to different business cultures.

Small-Scale Food Processing in Bangladesh

The sector. The increasingly urbanized population of Bangladesh has rapidly driven up demand for processed food (demand has risen at 32 percent annually). About 80 percent of food processing is done on a small scale in the home. Because this segment of the food processing sector receives limited or no policy support, it may not adapt to the dynamic market and regulatory context and remain competitive with the well-organized, large-scale food processing industry.

Main actors and their challenges. Faced with declining agricultural employment and limited rural nonfarm employment, the rural poor—mainly women lacking specific technical and business skills—have responded to growing demand for processed food by establishing home-based production units. Their job is complicated by a lack of credit facilities and by insufficient technical skills to meet hygiene standards. Their isolation and limited access to information have made it difficult to adjust to rapidly evolving consumer preferences and quality requirements in urban markets and to adopt changing processing and packaging techniques. The competitive large-scale processing industry places an additional strain on the financial sustainability of home-based businesses. The government emphasized agroprocessing in its 1999 agricultural policy but has not implemented actions to support small-scale processors. Public agricultural research on agroprocessing traditionally is weak, and NGOs provide virtually all of the support for the small-scale food processing sector.

Interaction mechanisms and innovation practices. In the early 1990s, a major international NGO identified small-scale food processing as an important livelihood option for poor people. The NGO's intervention was based primarily on the assumption that the poor had limited know-how for food preparation. Training in food processing became a mainstream development intervention that was then multiplied by local NGOs. For historical and ideological reasons, including their financial and technical dependence on the international NGO, local NGOs almost never engaged in other activities—especially in providing credit for food processing or offering training in the range of business and entrepreneurial skills that make the poor successful and innovative entrepreneurs. The public research system's weak tradition of agroprocessing research means that it has not established relations with small or industrial food processing firms. Similarly, interaction between NGOs and the research sector is absent. Finally, the social and physical separation of the dominant, urban, large-scale food processors and poor, rural, small-scale processors has hindered the creation of dynamic patterns of interaction and collaboration.

Enabling environment. In the policy environment, the small- and large-scale sectors are regarded differently. Tax incentives apply only to enterprises of large scale and scope; the small-scale sector benefits from none of these (or any other) incentives. Transport and market infrastructure have improved, yet many rural areas remain physically isolated from the main urban market in Dhaka.

Ways forward. As the large-scale industrial sector becomes increasingly competitive, the poverty reduction potential of the small-scale sector will be at risk if no substantial support is provided. Action could focus on supporting capacity in the small-scale sector to understand and benefit from links to markets, to understand product development and improve quality and safety characteristics, and to increase the scale of production (for example, through access to credit and collaboration with the large-scale sector). Strengthening of the

NGO sector is crucial for this effort to succeed. It will entail an improved understanding of the market and better coordination and networking capacity of NGOs with various actors, ranging from the research to industrial community. Fundamental improvements in small-scale processing will also likely require action from the public sector to enhance the enabling environment for small-scale production and to gear research toward processing and problem solving. Joint action on technical and research issues has the potential to benefit both large- and small-scale actors.

Medicinal Plants in India

The sector. India has a rich diversity of medically significant plants and very sophisticated indigenous medical traditions such as *ayurveda,* a holistic healing system that evolved in India 3,000–5,000 years ago. Medicinal plants traditionally have assumed great importance in the local health care systems of most poor people in India. During the late 1990s, exports of medicinal plants grew in response to increased international demand for a variety of herbal products, including medicines, health foods, and cosmetics. The greatly expanding sector faces many challenges, including (1) environmental degradation from destructive harvesting of plants, (2) the exploitation of poor plant collectors, (3) the sharing of benefits and profits between small and big companies, (4) regulatory and quality constraints in domestic and export markets, (5) international competition, and (6) intellectual property issues in light of India's World Trade Organization membership.

Main actors. The scale of the sector is enormous. It has a large number and diversity of actors with different interests, and policies influencing the sector are dispersed across many sector and ministerial portfolios. Tribal communities in forest areas do most of the plant collection and have few alternative livelihood opportunities. A large number of small, family-owned businesses manufacture and sell traditional herbal medicines locally, but they lack the research, manufacturing, and marketing skills to take advantage of opportunities in the domestic and international markets. In contrast, a small number of large Indian pharmaceutical companies have developed associated research, design, and marketing organizations with strong links to the international market. Their products have some resemblance to traditional herbal health care systems but are in fact increasingly developed through a hybrid of local, allopathic (conventional medicine, as opposed to homeopathic), and scientific means. The Medicinal Plants Board established by the government has not promoted sector coordination very effectively. In contrast, civil society organizations (NGOs, foundations) have been partially successful in coordination, albeit around traditional health care and rural development objectives rather than at the wider sector level.

Interaction mechanisms and innovation. Several attitudes and practices complicate interactions between the actors in the medicinal plants sector: (1) a long-established mistrust among public research organizations, the private sector, and NGOs; (2) the different philosophical foundations of scientific versus traditional medicine and the resistance to hybridize them; and (3) traditional rivalries between different branches of science concerned with medical plants (health, agriculture, forestry, and so on). The interaction around research and information is also very complex, because the vast knowledge about medicinal plants is held by different groups with dissimilar interests and philosophies. Local health practitioners and rural communities hold the ethnobotanical knowledge and concentrate on traditional health care, whereas research organizations in the public and private sector have the scientific knowledge and focus on product development and market share.

Enabling environment. By 1983 the Indian government had formally recognized the tremendous knowledge base and enormous potential of traditional Indian systems of medicine and supported the documentation and registration of this knowledge, especially knowledge of ayurveda. India's recently approved intellectual property rights system recognizes the rural population's entitlement to this traditional knowledge. The government also supported the elaboration of best practices for manufacturing traditional medicines.

Ways forward. The challenge for the sector is to create innovation capacity that simultaneously promotes sector growth while integrating economic, poverty reduction, and environmental concerns. Major tasks include (1) building the network of knowledge by fostering partnerships between different branches of science and between science and traditional health care systems; (2) rethinking the approach toward sector coordination (for example, by addressing the divides between rural development and business on the one hand, and between science and traditional health care on the other); and (3) redesigning research and training initiatives based on an exploration of the interfaces between traditional and scientific medicine.

Vanilla in India

The sector. In less than two decades, vanilla production in the State of Kerala has expanded from its very low and traditional production base to cultivation by 100,000 farm households. Exceptionally high global prices for green and cured vanilla beans during 2001–03 helped production expand, and India rapidly became a major player in the international vanilla market. Yet decline was equally rapid: by 2004 farmers faced sharply falling markets, and by 2005 the Indian vanilla sector seemed set for collapse. The sector's initial rapid expansion is explained by the efficiency with which different preexisting organizational forms enabled farmers to innovate in response to an emerging opportunity. In contrast, the sector's potential decline derives from institutional constraints on the emergence of new networks and innovations to cope with the uncertainties of the international vanilla market.

Main actors. The vanilla sector has developed over three periods in which different actors assumed different roles. In the early 1990s, a relatively minor government promotion campaign provided the initial impetus for farmers to produce vanilla. A large spice production and export company supplied planting material to farmers and to new farmer associations created to share knowledge about vanilla production and processing. Starting in 2000, the associations' role expanded to include negotiating prices and quality standards with traders and exploring and developing new markets and value-added products. Private firms were important purchasers of vanilla and also provided technical advice on production and processing. In 2004, when the world price for vanilla dropped dramatically, farmers could find no assistance to improve the profitability of their vanilla business, either from the government Spices Board or from India's extensive agricultural research system. That function was eventually filled by a new producer organization that has had some success in developing vanilla products for the domestic market.

Interaction mechanisms and innovation. Local attitudes and practices have been a source of success and failure. The tradition of farmer associations in Kerala, established earlier in the rubber sector, facilitated the creation of strong interaction among vanilla farmers around production and processing innovations. In contrast, interaction has been missing between major actors (farmers and the public research and support agencies, farmers and private companies) because of a lack of trust. This barrier has prevented the integration of different types of information (technical, market intelligence, socioeconomic) needed to innovate and maintain the international competitiveness of Indian vanilla.

Enabling environment. The enabling environment for innovation in the vanilla sector is broadly in place. Exports are widely promoted and Indian markets face sufficient competitive pressure to innovate. Research infrastructure is available to support innovation. But the sector has taken little advantage of this enabling environment.

Ways forward. The vanilla sector requires integrated efforts from public and private actors to deal with the extreme price uncertainties of the international vanilla market. This is a case where production and processing innovations would make Indian vanilla more competitive, marketing and quality branding could potentially attract a premium for Indian vanilla, and socioeconomic research could clarify the most effective strategies for farmers and traders. These results require the creation of an autonomous sector-coordinating body with the mandate to link the different groups (farmer associations, large commodity-trading companies, public research organizations, and the Spices Board of India) around these strategic issues. Unless this happens, the Indian vanilla sector is set to collapse in the near future.

Pineapple Export in Ghana

The sector. The growth of Ghanaian pineapple exports since the 1980s initially relied on a number of local entrepreneurs, low labor costs, suitable production conditions, and the proximity of the European market. The sector now faces many challenges: (1) increased competition from new pineapple-producing countries; (2) changing consumer preferences from traditional to new pineapple varieties; (3) the need to comply with increasingly regulated markets (for example, with EU food legislation); (4) the need to build and maintain a quality reputation for Ghanaian fruit in a heterogeneous production context (small-scale producers and large plantations); and (5) a shortage of technical staff with solid practical and managerial skills.

Main actors. Three types of export firms have been major players in the sector: (1) government- or donor-established private firms with a network of small producers, (2) corporations with their own plantations and processing plants, and (3) small companies with a smallholder production base. Most firms switched to new pineapple varieties and diversified away from fresh whole fruit into value-added processing, including cut and sliced fruit, juices, and certification for fair trade and organic produce. In seeking technology and know-how, they often developed their own individual expertise and research or relied upon foreign advisers. Although an industry-level association of Ghanaian pineapple exporters has the mandate to coordinate these approaches, it has not done so in practice. The private sector has been efficient in multiplying and distributing planting material of new varieties. The government has been relatively successful in establishing farmer-owned export companies as a means to link small producers to export markets, but its interventions in developing and supplying planting material have had limited success. Ghana's extensive agricultural research community has played only a minor role in the growth of the pineapple export sector.

Interaction mechanisms and innovation. The sector has been successful and continues to grow, yet it has not been very responsive to the changing export market. Relations among exporting firms are dominated by mistrust and technical self-sufficiency, as each firm works independently of its local competitors and carries out its own technical upgrading. The whole sector is in a vicious circle that hampers innovation: as long as the industry's demand for research is low, because of the assumption that scientists' work is commercially irrelevant, research agencies do not address topics that are significant for the sector, and universities are disconnected from the evolving research and management needs. Finally, the interaction between the public sector and exporting firms is limited to farmer training offered by the Ministry of Food and Agriculture.

Enabling environment. The government supports nontraditional exports— for example, through a free trade zone—and has established certification mechanisms for pineapple production systems. The Ministry of Food and Agriculture has supported training of pineapple growers to respond to pesticide management requirements. Other crucial efforts to ensure compliance with EU regulations, norms, and standards have relied on links with international organizations, including the German Agency for Technical Cooperation (GTZ), the U.S. Agency for International Development (USAID), and the Natural Resources Institute (NRI).

Ways forward. To remain internationally competitive, the Ghanaian pineapple sector needs to anticipate and adjust to the changing context and innovate on all fronts (production, postharvest, marketing, quality, and so on) at both the company and sector level. It must also remain inclusive of small producers. Achieving these goals requires more collaboration among exporting companies and between public and private research and training agencies. Key issues for the sector include achieving compliance with quality standards and certification and reorganizing national education and training in horticulture. Other actors, such as the Ghanaian pineapple exporters association and intermediary organizations (including NGOs), are likely to be essential in this coordination effort.

Cassava Processing in Ghana

The sector. The considerable investment in Ghana in food and industrial uses of cassava is illustrated by three approaches: (1) small-scale processing of *gari,* a grainlike, processed form of roasted, grated cassava; (2) the President's Special Initiative to create the Ayensu Starch Company Limited (ASCo) for producing cassava starch; and (3) the Sustainable Uptake of Cassava as an Industrial Commodity Project (SUCICP) for developing cassava-based industrial products such as flours, bakery products, and adhesives (conducted by the local Food Research Institute and its international partners, with financial support from DFID, the U.K. Department for International Development). The roles and interactions of three leading actors (the public sector, the private sector, and NGOs) in each approach can be related to the approach's success or failure in promoting innovation.

Main actors and their challenges. In the gari case, the public food science research agency played the traditional role of developing technology for processing. NGOs promoting small-scale processing focused on transferring the technology to self-help groups, which were at the end of the technology transfer chain and had no input in the previous stages. The private sector was involved in gari processing, although mostly independently of any of these initiatives.

In the ASCo case, the government encouraged the industrial use of cassava through a policy initiative. It played a dual role of (1) providing infrastructure and incentives to the private sector and (2) facilitating interaction between actors (for example, by creating a consortium of banks to finance ASCo). Research agencies stuck to their traditional technology function; their new cassava varieties, however, were relatively unsuitable to the production and processing context of farmers and ASCo. ASCo, unlike many other companies in Ghana, coordinated and supported a network of several thousand small-scale cassava producers.

In the SUCICP case, a research project was set up in which the private sector (and to a lesser extent NGOs) and the leading research agency were equal stakeholders. They collaborated on empirical questions about food science and also on system development and architecture. Although the researchers' scientific inputs were critical, the researchers also played a significant role in mediating between the actors along the value chain and monitoring (on a pilot scale at least) the functioning of the value chain.

Interaction mechanisms and innovation practices. In the gari case, interaction occurred through a classical top-down mode: scientists created technology for subsequent transfer to farmers by NGOs. In practice, the lack of interaction caused the initiative to fail.

In the ASCo case, the government successfully facilitated interaction between the banks and the new company and between farmers and the company. Good value chain linkages brought the company success at first, but weak knowledge-based interaction with agricultural research agencies seriously undermined ASCo's ability to innovate.

Success in the SUCICP case can be attributed to SUCICP's creation and nurturing of interactions between actors in the value chain, and between the value chain and the research system. It must be appreciated that this approach emerged after a series of traditional supply-led research projects headed by food scientists. Although these projects failed in a formal sense, they were needed to reveal the true nature of the research problem as one of creating and strengthening market and knowledge-based linkages. The new roles and practices of SUCICP greatly enhanced the public research agency's capacity to promote innovation in the sector.

Enabling environment. The enabling environment has been broadly supportive, especially in the President's Special Initiative. The government built appropriate infrastructure (roads, electricity, water supply facilities), facilitated the organization of farmer groups and their interaction with the private sector, and brought in a consortium of banks to satisfy financing requirements.

Ways forward. Further development of the cassava processing sector requires interventions that identify the real market potential, build upon the good practices from ASCo (infrastructure and incentives, links to financial services, coordination of small-scale producers) and SUCICP (collaboration between the private sector and research community along the value chain), and support innovation by rural microenterprises. The government and NGOs are in an ideal position to facilitate interaction among actors along the value chain and between private companies and research agencies. This interaction can occur around strategic problems such as the high cost of producing cassava starch, the need for more productive and better adapted cassava varieties and their adoption by farmers, and the search for new products and value chains.

Cassava Processing in Colombia

The sector. Cassava in Colombia has evolved in two decades from a traditional subsistence crop into an important agroindustrial crop because of its wide range of uses. The sector's success is the result of policy and institutional factors that have created a dense network between the main actors. The sector now faces great international competition, mainly related to the high costs of production and processing compared to other major global players such as Thailand.

Main actors. The roles of the actors in the sector have evolved over three periods. In 1983–92, the government's Integrated Rural Development Strategy promoted the industrialization of cassava as a source of rural employment and income. The National Association of Producers and Processors of Cassava was created to organize and support the commercialization of dried cassava. Fostered by protectionist policies, small-scale commercial processing of cassava (mainly for animal feed, flour, and starch) emerged and expanded with support from the International Center for Tropical Agriculture (CIAT) and the Colombian national agricultural research agency (now CORPOICA, the Colombian Corporation for Agricultural Research). CIAT's interdisciplinary research approach, market development orientation, and links with cooperative processing plants proved to be an advantage in bringing farmers into the process of industrialization at an early date. After undertaking a series of studies, including a needs analysis, CIAT targeted its cassava research toward dried cassava chips as an alternative source of energy in animal feed. The national research agency worked closely with CIAT.

In the early 1990s, structural adjustment and the drastic opening of the economy pulled policy makers' attention away from cassava. Privatization led to a drop in publicly funded agricultural research. Large imports of maize and starch undercut cassava production and the diversification of its uses. Small-scale producer cooperatives and small family businesses producing cassava-based food products, although struggling in the new market conditions, were the active players.

Since the mid-1990s, with the government's renewed interest in cassava, considerable research, policy, and coordination support yielded innovations in technology (mechanization from planting to processing, new varieties, and so forth) and industry (such as the use of forward contracts between buyers and sellers). Two new actors have played a significant role in innovation and sector coordination: the Latin American Consortium for Cassava Research and Development (CLAYUCA), a regional consortium of producer countries with a very strong connection to national and international research organizations (including CIAT), and the Association of Small-Scale Cassava Farmers from the Cordoba and Sucre Plains (APROYSA), which focuses on research in the animal feed industry.

Interaction mechanisms and innovation. Different local attitudes and practices helped to promote innovation in a socially inclusive way: (1) the willingness to explore different forms of partnership, (2) the tradition of cooperatives and industry associations, (3) the emphasis on the social and economic feasibility of a dualistic sector of small- and large-scale producers, and (4) the importance given to science and technology in sector development. These traditions allowed different forms of interaction and coordination to emerge, such as

(1) the partnership between CIAT, cooperative processing plants, and the Colombian national agricultural research organization; (2) the creation of an apex association to link cooperatives in processing and marketing innovations; and (3) the creation of a research-focused network comprising a regional consortium, the industry (with its small-scale farmer base), national and international research organizations, the government, and financial organizations—all linked to domestic, regional, and international markets.

Enabling environment. The Colombian government went to considerable effort to organize agricultural value chains and foster interaction and coordination between value chain agents. Cassava is considered part of the poultry and pig chains. In 2004 the government included cassava in its competitive call for research and development projects. Support for funding and value chains created a favorable enabling environment.

Ways forward. To secure its future growth, the Colombian cassava sector must reassess the market potential for various cassava-based products. Based on market research and demand, the sector should address the technical issues associated with high production and processing costs and develop new value-added products, such as cassava-based biofuels, biodegradable products, and pharmaceutical precursors. An important role for the government is to address policy and investment needs that have the potential to stimulate demand in domestic and international markets. To meet the technical challenges, research and training agencies must regain their strong innovation capacity and play a stronger and more integrated role in facilitating problem solving and collaboration across the actors in the value chain.

Cut Flowers in Colombia

The sector. From the 1960s, cut flowers rapidly became Colombia's top nontraditional export. By 2002 Colombia provided 15 percent of world cut flower exports and 75 percent of the cut flowers imported into the United States. Success was based on a natural comparative advantage for growing flowers and low production costs, but the rapidly evolving international flower export market has challenged the sector's capacity to remain financially sustainable without a more intensive process of innovation.

Main actors and their challenges. In the mid-1960s, many individual small-scale farmers with limited knowledge of floriculture started growing non-indigenous flowers (carnations and chrysanthemums) in open fields. Production depended greatly on imported inputs—plant stocks, fertilizers, pesticides, foreign technology, and expertise—and was delivered to Colombian export companies. The latter supplied primarily the United States market through well-developed distribution and marketing channels. From the late 1980s, Colombian export companies faced nontariff barriers in the United States as well as aggressive competition from other countries, including Ecuador, Kenya, and Ethiopia. New norms and standards (quality, environmental, and ethical) and a changing cost structure (rising labor costs, royalty payments to foreign intellectual property holders, and costs related to more capital-intensive cultivation) have further challenged the sector's financial sustainability. The sector's capacity to adapt to the evolving context is complicated by government neglect of local research (especially flower breeding capacity) for the flower sector.

Interaction mechanisms and innovation practices. Local adjustment strategies in the 1990s focused on alternative production and marketing mechanisms to strengthen the value chain. A move to collective production and marketing, along with a search for diversified distribution channels, was pursued by newly created vertically integrated firms and newly formed groups. The share of Colombian flower sales to supermarkets and retail chains in the United States reached 85 percent in the late 1990s (it was 13 percent in the 1970s). An exploration of new markets was accompanied by product diversification following changing consumer demand in the early 1980s. Varieties received brand names. Producers shifted from carnations and chrysanthemums to spray carnations and roses, and from stems to ready-made bouquets. Large- and medium-scale growers resorted to controlled growing conditions (greenhouses, drip irrigation, fertigation) and mainly produced roses. Small-scale farmers with 2 to 5 hectares started growing hydrangeas and calla lilies, which require less capital investment. Many traditional farmers, operating on only 0.5 to 1.5 hectares, failed to adapt to the new context and became agricultural laborers, despite government support of intermediary firms between smallholders and export markets. Continuous underinvestment in local research and technology for the flower sector fostered dependence on foreign technology and expertise and hampered local capacity to innovate. The attitudes and practices of the main flower export association, Asocolflores, as an organization dealing with international marketing issues, has hampered the organization's ability to bring research expertise to bear on the problems of the sector.

Enabling environment. The flower sector has evolved largely at arm's length from the government, with two obvious exceptions—the development of phytosanitary regulations and the government's support for coordinating the flower value chain. Public research has been negligible for a long time.

Ways forward. Stronger Colombian expertise in floriculture is urgently needed in the public and private sector if the cut flower industry is to anticipate and cope with change more efficiently and dynamically. The physical and emotional distance between the flower sector and research community must diminish. Strategic questions on sector development (such as how to satisfy changing international environmental standards or anticipate demand for organic products) could initiate collaboration between researchers and other sector actors. This requires coordination; the interaction mechanisms that have emerged for marketing may serve as a good practice and facilitate access to technology and research support. To promote this long-term process, government and industry should increasingly invest in floriculture-specific education and infrastructure, institutional development, and policy change.

CHAPTER FOUR

Innovation System Capacity: A Comparative Analysis of Case Studies

This chapter analyzes the case studies from an innovation systems perspective. The analysis follows the four main elements of the analytical framework developed in chapters 2 and 3:

- *Actors and their roles.* Who were the key actors associated with each case study, what roles did they play, and what were the strengths and weaknesses of these roles in promoting innovation?
- *Attitudes and practices.* What attitudes and practices were characteristic of the actors in each case study? How did these attitudes and practices help to promote (or impede) innovation?
- *Patterns of interaction.* What patterns of interaction existed in each case study, and to what extent did they strengthen the innovation capacity?
- *The enabling environment for innovation.* How did the science and technology, fiscal, and legal policy contexts influence the innovation ability of the system?

ACTORS, THEIR ROLES, AND THE ATTITUDES AND PRACTICES THAT SHAPE THEIR ROLES

The case studies highlight the diversity of actors associated with the development of each sector and the innovations that have taken place. The actors come from the entire spectrum of public and private actors in the economy. Because the case studies provide a historical perspective on the development of the sectors, they also reveal how different groups of actors can become important or take on new roles at different times (see annex C, table C.1, for a detailed summary). In many of the case studies, the only actors doing anything significant in the early stages of sector development were entrepreneurs, who innovated in response to opportunities. In other cases, notably cassava processing in Colombia and Ghana, the government was more active, orchestrating the sector's take-off by providing research and other support. In exploring these issues, it becomes apparent that roles cannot necessarily be discussed independently of the attitudes and practices that inform or shape them.

Government

In the *government-orchestrated cases,* the government's role was obviously important from the beginning. In the *entrepreneur-driven cases,* often the sector came to the attention of the government only after it had started to take off, and the government did not intervene until the sector started to stagnate or encounter major disruptions.[5]

It is quite difficult to distinguish between *government action designed to provide an enabling environment* for the sector and *specific support for innovation in that sector* (box 4.1), although dedicated research programs are examples of specific support. Often the government may have been investing in agricultural research and training and subsequently established a *dedicated scheme* or *pilot initiative* to orchestrate the sector's take-off. Although *research support* was a common form of government intervention, especially to foster the emergence of a new sector, often it was integrated poorly with initiatives of other actors in the sector and thus ineffective. Sometimes the government has *provided trained personnel* for emerging agroindustries; more often, however, university curricula have failed to keep up with the needs of a thriving agroindustrial sector.

In Ghana, under the president's special scheme for cassava, the government *provided infrastructure*—roads, power, and other utilities—to encourage the private sector to establish starch factories. Duly established, these factories almost immediately ran into trouble. With limited connections to research and other support for innovation, they failed to innovate in response to highly competitive international starch markets. In contrast, the Colombian government recognized its role in *encouraging linkages* between actors in the cassava sector and put special measures in place to do so. The government then used a range of interventions to create a dense network of research, training, and private organizations to sustain a dynamic process of innovation.

The Private Sector

Private organizations play a central role in all of the case studies and can be disaggregated into several types.

- *Microentrepreneurs* include farmers producing commodities (such as Indian vanilla farmers, who proved to be an important source of production innovations) and nonfarm entrepreneurs (such as small-scale food processors in Bangladesh, who responded to the demand for snack food and processed foods).
- *Companies,* from very small to very large, acting on their own or in partnership with government, were central to the emergence of several sectors. For example, Bangladeshi companies recognized international market opportunities for shrimp and set up processing and export facilities. Indian companies developed new herbal remedies and marketing strategies aimed at emerging middle-class consumers. Companies were featured in some government-led scenarios (starch companies participated in government efforts to develop Ghana's cassava sector, for example).
- *Private advisory services* introduced production and postproduction innovations that helped sectors respond to changing standards and norms—instituting Global Partnership for Safe and Sustainable Agriculture (EurepGAP)[6]

for pineapple in Ghana and HACCP for shrimp in Bangladesh, for example. Advisory services not only supported technical upgrading and trouble-shooting for companies; they also linked companies to early information on changes in standards and norms to help them innovate on time.

- *Private input supply companies* provided technology so farmers could respond to new opportunities or requirements: the private sector initially supplied some of the planting material for vanilla in India, flower producers in Colombia obtained new varieties through licensing agreements with foreign companies, and a private tissue culture facility in Ghana provided planting material for a new Costa Rican pineapple variety that was in high demand.
- *Farmer associations* and *producer-owned companies and cooperatives* have played an important role as well. Farmer associations in India became an important conduit for sharing knowledge of vanilla production technology among farmers, negotiating prices with traders, and determining quality standards. In Colombia, farmer associations proved instrumental in providing production and processing technology that was critical for upgrading the cassava sector. Vanillco, a producer-owned company in India, developed product innovations to foster a domestic vanilla market in response to low international market prices. The community-owned medicinal plant company, Gram Mouliga, was a marketing innovation to bypass the exploitative practices of middlemen and traders.
- *Industry associations* have been important in strengthening marketing arrangements and in political lobbying, but they often fail to expand or change these roles where necessary and play a more proactive role in enabling innovation (see the examples in the discussion of coordinating bodies later in this chapter).

The private sector can also play a significant role in research programs to support innovation. In Ghana, a *research partnership* between the Food Research Institute and companies using cassava as a raw material resulted in organizational innovations that improved the functioning of the value chain and in product innovations to create new products and improve product quality. *Private research capacity* developed by the flower industry association in Colombia reduced reliance on varieties from foreign companies. Similar capacity in a Colombian subsidiary of an Italian firm gave the Colombian firm an advantage over its competitors, whose breeding programs were located abroad. Research expertise in India's large herbal drug companies has inspired product and marketing innovations.

Coordinating Bodies

The need for interaction, collaboration, and coordination is apparent in most of the sectors studied. Most case studies documented the existence of a range of organizations established to coordinate various activities, including marketing, access to technical and financial capacity or services, assistance in meeting or setting quality standards, and political lobbying. Coordinating bodies consisted of public organizations (such as the Medicinal Plants Board in India), NGOs or foundations, industry associations (such as those established around the cassava processing sector in Colombia or the shrimp industry in Bangladesh), and consortia of private and public organizations (such as CLAYUCA).

Some sectors clearly require coordinating bodies, yet those bodies are absent. Many coordinating bodies in the case studies were weak at promoting innovation. Either they emphasized a limited set of alternative activities, such as political lobbying in the case of shrimp in Bangladesh, or their activities and expertise were limited in scope, which was the case with Asocolflores, the Colombian Association of Flower Exporters. Asocolflores developed when successful marketing was viewed as the key source of competitiveness, and it did not cultivate relationships with research organizations to foster more knowledge-intensive innovation throughout the sector. In contrast, CLAYUCA, the successful regional coordinating body based in Colombia, had a very strong research orientation arising from the national and international research organizations that helped to establish it. CLAYUCA played the role of facilitator for cassava research and development, fostering collaboration among the actors and identifying organizational and technical bottlenecks requiring intervention.

Sometimes NGOs assume the role of a coordinating body. An Indian NGO, the Foundation for the Revitalisation of Local Health Traditions (FRLHT), with an interest in strengthening the material, human, and knowledge base of traditional medicines, became a successful coordinating body by building partnerships based on shared concerns related to medicinal plants, local health care traditions, and the conservation of biodiversity. These partnerships involved a range of government departments (responsible for forests, various aspects of research, and health care) as well as other NGOs.

NGOs

NGOs played different roles in the case studies, serving as coordinating bodies (discussed earlier), technology transfer agents, or intermediary organizations.

NGOs as technology transfer agents. In several cases, NGOs acted as technology transfer agents (sometimes because other providers were missing), but they tended to fail in this role. Although NGOs in Bangladesh and Ghana focused on improving the technical skills of food processors, the key constraint for the small and poor processors was not their lack of skill but rather their weak links to information, technology, and services such as credit. Even when NGOs developed a business model with self-help groups, the model was imposed so strictly that businesses lacked the flexibility to meet challenges with marketing and other innovations. In each case, poor people needed an intermediary organization to facilitate or broker their access to knowledge and services—a skill that many NGOs must strengthen if they are to assume this role.

NGOs as intermediary organizations. Intermediary organizations may pursue some of the same functions as coordinating bodies, but they may also have a special role in promoting social as well as economic objectives through better interaction between public and private organizations. Intermediary organizations that specifically addressed business and social objectives were missing from most sectors investigated, signaling a major weakness in pro-poor innovation capacity. One exception was in Ghana, where Technoserve, a specialized NGO, acted as an intermediary in the pineapple sector. Technoserve assisted export companies in developing a network of smallholder organic pineapple growers and accessing technical assistance for growers and companies. It also assisted the companies in gaining certification as exporters of organic pineapple products and in preparing business plans to obtain loans from Ghana's Export Development and Investment Fund.

Financial Organizations

Much greater consideration needs to be given to financing innovation, and financing organizations need to play a greatly expanded role. The financing of innovation did not feature strongly in most of the case studies, which is symptomatic of the fact that financing and financial organizations usually are forgotten in the analysis, design and implementation of interventions that aim to strengthen innovation capacity. There were some exceptions: Technoserve helped provide access to finance for Ghanaian pineapple producers; in Colombia, a new form of financing—based on futures trading—was critical for expanding cassava production so the processing industry could run more efficiently. More commonly, the sectors studied were limited by poor access to credit, particularly for poor entrepreneurs who wanted to launch and sustain businesses. In Bangladesh, not only did most NGOs (the main form of support for the food processing sector) lack credit programs, but many microcredit organizations serving the poor did not recognize food processing as a viable lending option.

International Actors

International actors, including donors, international research organizations, and trade associations of international companies, are often vital in providing the initial technical foundation for new innovation systems and in improving the sustainability of these systems. The international actors in the case studies played three kinds of roles: supporting technology development, improving marketing, and enhancing the environmental and social sustainability of the subsector innovations.

Support for technology development was the most central role. In Ghana's cassava industrialization program, DFID sustained a technical support program for 10 years to build the foundation for industrial uses of cassava. Similarly, CIAT played a strong initial role in Colombia in providing technologies for novel industrial uses of cassava. Donors were instrumental in helping Ghanaian pineapple producers to meet new European quality standards. With regard to social sustainability, DFID support was also instrumental in linking small-scale farmers to markets in the Ghana cassava case. The clearest example of supporting environmental sustainability occurred in the Bangladesh shrimp case, in which donors supported technologies to reduce environmental risks.

ATTITUDES AND PRACTICES

Attitudes and established practices strongly define how organizations respond to changing conditions. This section reviews how attitudes and practices define the roles that actors can take and the patterns of interaction in which they can engage.

Attitudes and practices define which roles organizations can take. In some instances, an organization's original set of goals and skills interferes with its capacity to innovate when conditions change. As mentioned earlier, the traditional role of Asocolflores was to support export marketing. When increasing competition revealed the need for research to help the industry innovate, the association encountered great difficulty in supporting the development of research capacity for the cut flower industry. Not only did Asocolflores lack experience—its technology was licensed from foreign companies—but it also lacked the trust of the local research community. Relations with local researchers had to be developed before the association's need for research could be met.

Attitudes and practices lead to interaction for the wrong reason. In some instances, organizations' motives for interaction may be inconsistent with the goals of the organization promoting the interaction. For example, the NGO that provided pioneering support for small-scale food processing in Bangladesh subsequently funded and trained local NGOs to step in and help poor people adopt food processing as a livelihood. The international NGO established a knowledge-sharing network—a Forum for Food Processing Enterprise Development (FFPED)—to promote learning and strengthen the capacity to support small-scale food processing among local NGOs. The FFPED failed, however, because most NGOs joined to gain access to funding from the international NGO.

Attitudes and practices lead to weak interaction among actors. Organizations may fail to meet new objectives that require interaction because their traditional attitudes and practices prevent interaction. India's central government set up the Medicinal Plants Board to coordinate all matters relating to medicinal plants by fostering collaboration across government departments and between the government, private sector, and NGOs. Established as a government body, the board inherited the very bureaucratic traditions that had prevented the integration of different organizations and interests related to medicinal plants in the first place. In particular, the board's lack of autonomy prevented it from exercising the flexibility and responsiveness needed in a successful coordinating body. Another example is the FRLHT. Its efforts to serve as a coordinating body have been attenuated by its ideology, which inhibits interaction with business and scientific organizations, although it has been quite successful in coordinating the actions of rural development agencies.

Attitudes and practices support good forms of interaction. In contrast to the cases cited earlier are cases in which attitudes and practices promoted good forms of interaction. In the case of vanilla in India, a tradition of farmer associations in the rubber sector had prepared farmers for associative modes of operation, which were important in spreading vanilla production innovations between farmers. The Colombia case studies also highlighted how associations have been important in promoting innovation.

Attitudes and practices shape public and private sector interaction. In many developing countries, the public and private sectors have developed in spite of rather than because of each other. The insularity of the public and private sectors becomes a serious constraint to innovation—for example, when the private sector could step in to disseminate new technologies produced in the public sector but is prevented from doing so through lack of access or lack of awareness. This problem is reinforced by an ivory tower culture in many research organizations, which diverts attention from resolving the problems of the sector to discovering new knowledge.

Attitudes must change to promote interaction by multiple actors. All of the actors in a sector need to change their attitudes and practices to support a continuous process of innovation. Very different attitudes toward partnerships and other forms of collaboration, and toward research and knowledge generation, are needed, along with changed practices to support those activities. For example, industry must recognize that the knowledge-intensity of agriculture implies that research can no longer be dismissed as irrelevant, and industry must identify ways to articulate the kinds of research it needs. In turn, research organizations must recognize that they are not the only ones that can change the face of agriculture.

Attitudes toward learning influence success. Learning within a network of actors builds the network's capacity to innovate, survive, and move forward, whereas otherwise the sector would die. Few case studies illustrated that experimentation and learning were at the core of the innovation process, but when they were, they clearly underpinned success; a good example is the experiments with partnership types in the Colombian cassava sector.

Attitudes toward poverty influence pro-poor innovation. A number of cases provided examples of pro-poor innovation. Some innovations allowed the poor to participate in the value chain, such as the use of networks of small-scale pineapple producers in Ghana and milk producers in Bangladesh; others made the participation of the poor less exploitative, such as the community-owned company for procuring and marketing medicinal plants in India. These innovations arose because being socially inclusive was part of the agenda of the organization involved. Incentives could be provided to encourage these perspectives.

Patterns of Interaction

The case studies provide examples of sectors in which interaction between actors fostered innovation, but more commonly they show how a characteristic lack of interaction prevented innovation. Types of interaction are described in the sections that follow and summarized in table 4.1 for each case study (see annex C, table C.3, for a detailed summary).

Farmer-to-Farmer Interaction

The vanilla case study in India provides a good example of how farmer-to-farmer interaction can promote the spread of production and postharvest innovations. In this particular case, farmers in Kerala had a lot of experience with farmer associations, which proved to be a good way for organizing and facilitating interactions. In Colombia, cassava cooperatives and associations encouraged farmer-to-farmer interaction, although it was more to organize the value chain than to promote innovation. In the remaining cases, farmer-to-farmer interaction, while undoubtedly occurring, was not organized in any way and would almost certainly have benefited from mechanisms to strengthen it.

Interactions of Businesses with the Poor and the Environment

Several examples of interaction between companies and the poor appeared in the case studies. The pineapple case in Ghana shows how these interactions helped develop win-win, pro-poor business models that were successful in terms of the profit perspective of the company as well as the income-earning perspective of the poor. These interactions helped companies comply with standards and norms that suited smallholder production systems. In most cases, however, these interactions were missing, and NGOs could have played a much stronger role in facilitating them. The food processing sector in Bangladesh is an example of this failure, particularly because of the large number of poor small-scale producers, the emergence of an organized large-scale processing sector, and sector support measures that seem to increase competition between the two.

Company-to-Company Interaction

This form of interaction rarely occurred in the case studies in the absence of mechanisms such as an industry association or a public coordinating body. Even when it did occur, companies collaborated only in political lobbying or coordinating the value chain and not in technical upgrading and other forms of innovation. Yet the case studies make it apparent that innovation through company-to-company interaction is becoming one of the most important

Table 4.1 Interaction Patterns in Support of Innovation

Sector and country	Main types of interaction
Shrimp, Bangladesh	*Company-to-company:* through sector association, but focused on political lobbying *Technology transfer:* through donor and government technical assistance projects *Missing interactions:* public-private sector partnerships
Small-scale food processing, Bangladesh	*Technology transfer:* through NGO-led technology transfer activities *Top down:* through policy formulation process *Missing interactions:* between business and representatives of the poor and the environment
Medicinal plants, India	*Multiactor interaction:* through public coordinating body, but not very effective, and through NGO with partnership as a core approach *Missing interactions:* multiactor interactions that are inclusive of public, private, and NGO actors
Vanilla, India	*Farmer-to-farmer:* through farmer associations *Missing interactions:* multiactor interaction and public-private research including farmers
Pineapple, Ghana	*Companies and the representatives of the poor and the environment:* through export business models that rely on smallholder production *Missing interactions:* multiactor interactions and public-private interactions on both research and training
Cassava processing, Ghana	*Technology transfer:* through research and extension *Public-private partnership:* through a pilot project that created a value chain and the linkages needed to integrate research support *Missing interactions:* multiactor interaction
Cassava, Colombia	*Public-private partnership:* through research approaches that encouraged experimentation with partnership and other forms of collaboration *Multiactor interaction:* through regional consortia *Company-to-company:* through commodity-based associations
Cut flowers, Colombia	*Company-to-company:* through an industry association principally established to work on marketing issues *Missing interactions:* public-private partnerships in research and training; multiactor interaction

Source: Authors.

needs in many sectors. Unless sectors such as shrimp in Bangladesh, pineapple in Ghana, cassava products in Ghana and Colombia, and vanilla in India can respond with agility to changing market demands—which will require coordinated changes across the whole sector—they will be driven out of business by competing countries with lower prices, better quality products, and novel value-added products. The cut flower sector in Colombia has been somewhat better at promoting company-to-company interaction. These relationships are part of a large network of connections that the sector is developing to allow it to become much more agile and responsive.

An important finding from the case studies is that even where competitive pressures provide all of the incentives for companies to interact and innovate, they do not result in sufficient interaction. Attitudes and practices embedded in the business culture of many sectors and countries inform these patterns of behavior, which greatly restrict the range of issues on which companies will collaborate. This constraint must be addressed in the medium and long term if company-to-company interaction is to be strengthened and a continuous process of innovation enabled.

Technology Transfer Interaction

Technology transfer interactions were observed in a number of the case studies, and problems associated with this approach have been well documented elsewhere. In the cassava processing case from Ghana, a new cassava variety was developed especially for processing and released by a public agricultural research organization. Only after release did the industry discover that the variety was unsuitable for processing. Such occurrences are common where the classic research and extension system remains in place, but they also appear in cases where NGOs have developed technology transfer programs, as in Bangladesh (food processing) and Ghana (cassava). Since NGOs generally have a good pro-poor focus, strengthening their capacity to promote innovation in ways that rely on better patterns of interaction rather than on technology transfer alone would seem to make a lot of sense.

Public-Private Partnerships to Improve Interaction with Research

Despite the fact that research remains one of the most important sources of knowledge that farmers and companies need in order to innovate, their interaction with research organizations is usually very weak, for three main reasons. First, commonly used capacity development approaches such as the NARS model have stressed the separation of research from related areas of economic activity. Second, enterprises have usually emerged and taken off independently of research support and have never built up linkages and relationships with research organizations. Third, few companies have strong formal technical skills and therefore lack a common language with researchers. Where companies do have strong technical expertise, they feel it is superior to that of the public sector, which they regard as too academic. The net result of this perception is that research plays a small part in the company's innovation activities.

In the case studies, when special arrangements were in place to foster collaboration between researchers and entrepreneurs, research was more effective in promoting innovation. One mechanism used to foster collaboration was partnerships (for example, in Colombia and Ghana on cassava), based on the recognition that the main research task was to investigate how to create or strengthen value chains and identify ways in which research organizations could support innovation at different points in the value chain. Another mechanism—farmer and industry associations—helped farmers deal with specific technical problems by linking with research organizations. Most often, however, the case studies highlight that this form of interaction is absent and remains a major constraint to enabling innovation.

Interactions of Multiple Actors

It has already been argued that innovation requires a dense network of interaction. Networks might crystallize around different innovation tasks at different times. In the case of medicinal plants in India and cassava processing in Colombia, interactions of multiple actors were important for the development of the sector. Coordinating bodies were established in both cases to foster the interaction. The establishment of such bodies is an important intervention. Their role must be given careful thought, however, and their governance must account for the needs of the sector, its political economy, and the institutional setting in which it must operate.

In some of the case studies, the lack of a coordinating body prevented innovation. To cope with fluctuating market prices, for example, the vanilla sector in India needed to find a way to compete with lower-priced competitors. The sector required accurate information about market prices (held by the public Spices Board); information about production costs (held by the local agricultural university); expertise to improve productivity (held in different public research organizations); information about advanced vanilla processing technology (held by private companies); coordinated efforts across the sector to improve the quality and brand image of Indian vanilla (all actors); and learning to cope with volatile markets for high-value spices (all actors). At present there is such animosity between the actors that they find it difficult to communicate with each other and certainly would not collaborate in ways that the sector demands. Without a mechanism such as a coordinating body to develop more productive forms of interaction, the vanilla sector in Kerala may well collapse.

THE ENABLING ENVIRONMENT

Several elements of the enabling environment can be observed in the case studies. In Colombia, cassava was eligible for competitive funds for research and development; in Ghana, farmer associations were established and involved in developing organizational innovation needed to address export opportunities; in India, the existing organizational structure of the farm community helped the vanilla crop to grow to important levels quickly (although it could not prevent it from declining). In the medicinal plants case, the adoption of a new intellectual property rights regime in India will certainly help the national industry to strengthen its position while still recognizing the rights of the rural population.

As shown in Bangladesh, traditional instruments such as tax relief for innovation investments work better for the more formal, larger-scale sector than for informal small and medium enterprises or the farm community. While standardization and certification have been pursued in several cases, including pineapple in Ghana, the capacity to enforce these systems is limited, leaving the regulatory efforts in a vacuum.

One of the more effective elements of the innovation environment in the case studies appears to be the encouragement of value chain coordination. Value chain coordination leads to stronger interactions, greater agreement on challenges to a sector, and greater willingness to pursue innovation, as shown for flowers and cassava in Colombia. The similarity of value chain and innovation system approaches thus can be pursued one step further: many of the actors are the same, but the type of interaction is different. Often market-based linkages are developed without sufficient consideration of the knowledge-based linkages required for innovation. The value chain approach provides a useful organizational principle for identifying the key actors in the production-to-consumption chain. However, the actors, their roles, and the types of interaction need to be analyzed from an innovation systems perspective. The potential synergy of combining the effective market-based and knowledge-based interactions needed for innovation in the value chain could form the basis for a powerful new form of intervention. The Colombian cases, and to some extent the cassava case in Ghana, would seem to provide evidence for the potential of this approach.

The most salient finding in many of the cases is that the innovation system could not take advantage of the existing enabling environment. The capacity to enforce standards effectively or implement a certification system was absent, or the ability to submit competitive proposals to a grant fund was deficient. Owing to this lack of capacity, the actors in the sector did not benefit from the support that the enabling environment could offer. It was not the enabling environment but weak patterns of interaction—and the attitudes and practices that fostered those patterns—that created the major bottleneck in the innovation process. In many cases, improvements in the enabling environment will be effective only if they are combined with activities to strengthen other aspects of innovation capacity, particularly the patterns of interaction of the main actors in the innovation system.

SUMMARY OF THE ANALYSIS OF INNOVATION CAPACITY IN THE CASE STUDIES

Evidence from the case studies (table 4.2) suggests that the patterns of interaction necessary to create dynamic systems of innovation are frequently absent. All too often farmers, microentrepreneurs, and companies have not been part of the network of research, training, and development organizations required to bring about a continuous process of innovation. The problem is not that candidate organizations for this network are absent. Usually many of these organizations are present, but they are not playing the required roles, or they have not formed the relationships required to support the dialogue that leads to fruitful interaction, learning, and innovation. Reluctance to form such relationships is reinforced by deep-seated behavioral patterns and mistrust, which originate in the roles these organizations played in earlier, less dynamic, and less challenging economic environments.

Evidence that attitudes and practices are a key bottleneck comes from the fact that strong incentives to innovate, arising from exposure to highly competitive markets, have rarely been sufficient to induce new patterns of collaboration. This lack of interaction has several results:

■ *Limited access to new knowledge.* Farmers, microentrepreneurs, and companies are cut off from the sources of knowledge they need to solve problems, create new products and processes, and thus cope and compete.
■ *Weak articulation of demand for research and training.* Policies, training curricula, and research efforts by public bodies are disconnected from the needs and agenda of the sector.
■ *Weak or absent technological learning.* Opportunities to master new skills through collaboration with others are limited.
■ *Weak or absent institutional learning at the company/farmer/entrepreneur level and at the sector level.* There are only restricted opportunities to build knowledge about how to innovate in response to rapidly changing conditions.
■ *Weak sector upgrading.* Organizations are ineffective at dealing with changing trade standards or developing a national brand image.
■ *Weak integration of social and environmental concerns into sector planning and development.* The sector is usually concerned with production and profit but gives little attention to the environmental and social conditions in which it operates. This attitude may create environmental problems and social tension and may reduce access to export markets.
■ *Weak connection to sources of financing for innovation.* Innovation is not only about new knowledge and new practices but about investing in the capacity to apply novelty on a large scale. The innovation process may fail because there are no financial means to introduce change on a large scale.

Table 4.2 Summary of the Analysis of Innovation Systems in the Case Studies

Sector and country	Roles	Patterns of interaction	Attitudes and practices	Enabling environment for innovation
Shrimp, Bangladesh	**Strengths:** Private-sector-led industrial development. Government providing infrastructure. NGOs supporting farmer welfare. **Weaknesses:** Industry association's role restricted to political lobbying. Research organizations not addressing sector problems. No effective sector-coordinating body.	**Strengths:** Well-developed value chain. **Weaknesses:** Poor links between farmers and companies and national research organizations. Poor links to export nations and international bodies dealing with standards.	**Strengths:** Strong market orientation. **Weaknesses:** Industry associations lack tradition of activities related to research and technical upgrading. Tradition of mistrust between public and private sectors and of mistrust between companies. Social exclusion. Tradition of non-compliance with food and environmental standards.	**Strengths:** Numerous technical assistance programs. **Weaknesses:** Technical assistance not focusing on developing the networks needed to underpin future innovation capacity. Inadequacy of research and training support.
Small-scale food processing, Bangladesh	**Strengths:** Many entrepreneurial households. NGO focus on sector as a development entry point. **Weaknesses:** Very limited government role, with no research support. NGOs focused on limited set of interventions, mainly technical training. NGOs not acting as intermediary organizations to better connect and integrate the poor.	**Strengths:** None. **Weaknesses:** Poor households not connected to sources of information on changing markets. Support networks needed to develop, produce, and market new products.	**Strengths:** Pro-poor agenda of NGOs. **Weaknesses:** Tradition of not lending to small-scale food processing sector. NGO dealing with small-scale food processing not working on microfinance. Technology transfer traditions of NGOs. NGO networks more interested in access to funds rather than research, learning, upgrading.	**Strengths:** None. **Weaknesses:** No policy support for the sector.

Medicinal plants, India	**Strengths:** Well-developed herbal remedies industry. Recognized traditional practitioners. Research and training organizations. NGO. **Weaknesses:** Sector-coordinating body ineffective.	**Strengths:** Pockets of successful interaction in rural development and corporate subsectors. **Weaknesses:** Integration of rural development and corporate sector networks at strategic points. Multiactor linkages for sectorwide activities poorly developed.	**Strengths:** Pro-poor and pro-environment agenda of NGOs. **Weaknesses:** Ideological and philosophical incompatibility between major stakeholder groups. Bureaucratic tendencies of sector-coordinating body.	**Strengths:** Investments in research and training and sector coordination. **Weaknesses:** Institutional setting negates research and training and sector coordination measures.
Vanilla, India	**Strengths:** Active farmer and producer association. **Weaknesses:** Ineffective commodity board. No relevant public research. Absence of intermediary organization.	**Strengths:** Farmer-to-farmer interaction helping to spread production and processing innovations. **Weaknesses:** No linkages between farmers and research organizations. No multiactor linkages for sectorwide activities.	**Strengths:** Strong tradition of associative action by farmers. **Weaknesses:** High levels of mistrust between all actors in sector.	**Strengths:** Progressive export promotion policies in place, but little to actively enable innovation. **Weaknesses:** Lack of investment in appropriate research and training.
Pineapple, Ghana	**Strengths:** Active private sector. NGO intermediary organization. **Weaknesses:** Limited role of public research. Absence of sector-coordinating body.	**Strengths:** Companies and networks of smallholder producers. **Weaknesses:** Companies and research and training organizations. Multiactor interactions for sectorwide upgrading.	**Strengths:** Inclusiveness of small farmers and small companies. **Weaknesses:** Tension between public and private sector on research/technical assistance. Weak tradition of companies collaborating on sectorwide upgrading.	**Strengths:** Financing mechanisms for export-oriented industry development. **Weaknesses:** Lack of appropriate research and training arrangements.

(continued)

Table 4.2 Continued

Sector and country	Roles	Patterns of interaction	Attitudes and practices	Enabling environment for innovation
Cassava processing, Ghana	**Strengths:** Relevant public research in pilot project. Active industry. **Weaknesses:** Much public research inappropriate. NGO focusing on technology transfer. No intermediary organization to include the poor.	**Strengths:** Coalition of research and industry actors seen in pilot project. **Weaknesses:** Technology transfer in the usual way (linking research to farmers and industry).	**Strengths:** New ways of doing research with the private sector seen in pilot project. **Weaknesses:** Research system capacity development traditions that have isolated research from relevant areas of economic activity.	**Strengths:** Investments in food research. **Weaknesses:** Training provision poorly linked to recent sector developments and needs.
Cassava, Colombia.	**Strengths:** Public research support, but also international research center with "research focus on market development. **Weaknesses:** Inconsistent role of public agencies.	**Strengths:** Existence of multiple forms of collaboration. Focus on value chain development and innovation and upgrading. **Weaknesses:** Coordination of activities across different value chain could be strengthened further.	**Strengths:** Inclusiveness of farmer association and of arrangements for access to credit. Learning from previous experiences with other crops. Strong research tradition. Smallholders also involved in some of the processing, such as the drying process, and in the fermented starches industry.	**Strengths:** Support for research and training. **Weaknesses:** Instability with frequent changes in government support for research.

Cut flowers, Colombia	**Strengths:** Industry and producer associations. **Weaknesses:** No public research and training organization working on cut flowers. Industry and producer associations tend to focus on development of the value chain and until recently had no role in supporting research. Universities have only limited roles in training researchers and practitioners.	**Strengths:** Well-developed value chain. **Weaknesses:** Collaboration between actors in the sector and between the sector and research organizations in Colombia is rather weak.	**Strengths:** Tradition of industry association. **Weaknesses:** Historical tendency to secrecy among flower growers and lack of a collaborative tradition. Marketing tradition in exporter association ignored development of research expertise.	**Strengths:** Allowed sector to take advantage of tie-ups with foreign companies, although this limited innovation in the long term. **Weaknesses:** Absence of research and training support for the sector.

Source: Authors.

CHAPTER FIVE

Reviewing the Innovation Systems Concept in Light of the Case Studies

This chapter uses examples from the case studies to illustrate some key features of innovation that were set out in the analytical framework. These are presented to illustrate the robustness and potential of the innovation systems concept as a basis for diagnostic and intervention frameworks. The chapter also draws together some of the major findings from the study, outlines the key contemporary innovation challenges, and presents the implications for interventions that seek to strengthen innovation capacity. It concludes by reviewing the types of interventions that commonly have been used and examines their limitations from an innovation systems perspective.

THE NATURE OF CONTEMPORARY AGRICULTURAL CHALLENGES

A common theme from the case studies is the critical *evolutionary* and *integrated* nature of contemporary challenges and opportunities facing agriculture. These challenges and opportunities are evolutionary in the sense that they emerge in unpredictable ways (as with changing trade standards or consumer preferences) and that dealing with these new conditions often requires new alliances and patterns of collaboration. Challenges and opportunities are integrated in the sense that actions along the value chain cannot be dealt with independently of each other and cannot be addressed without considering social and economic factors. The implication is that interaction, collaboration, and coordination are increasingly important ingredients of economic success.

Evolutionary Nature of Challenges

Evolutionary challenges are strongly related to changing market regulation, changing patterns of competition, and consumer preferences, but challenges also reflect changes unrelated to markets, such as emerging crop and animal diseases, climatic variability, and natural calamities such as the Asian tsunami.

Regulation, standards, and norms. Sanitary and phytosanitary standards for shrimp from Bangladesh or pineapples from Ghana are continuously made more stringent in response to food safety concerns in Europe and North America. Ethical standards, such as the working conditions of employees and the use of child labor, are major concerns in the flower industry. A notable feature of compliance with changing quality standards (physical, social, or environmental) is that compliance often requires a sectorwide approach, because national reputation greatly influences buying patterns in major markets in Europe and North America. These pressures to innovate call for stronger patterns of interaction.

Competition. Many of the case studies illustrate that sectors are facing strong competition, often because of new entrants with lower production costs or other advantages. The Bangladesh shrimp sector faces competition in the U.S. market from Chile, Ecuador, and Brazil and is struggling to find an adequate response. In response to competition from Kenya and Ecuador, Colombia's cut flower sector has developed value-added products such as bouquets and diversified into products for the local market. Cassava processing in Colombia and Ghana suffers from relatively low cassava yields, indicating that the processing sector must increase productivity or develop value-added products such as high-quality starches for the confectionary and pharmaceutical industries. The trend toward a country-to-country pattern of competition for a share of an export market, rather than a pattern of individual companies competing with one another, increases the pressure to collaborate.

Changing consumer preferences. A major concern for the Colombian flower industry has been to keep up with shifts in demand preferences. Initially standard carnations and chrysanthemums were popular, then preferences shifted to spray carnations and roses and later to foliage plants. The challenge has been to access new planting material, especially because Colombia had practically no flower research and breeding capability and licensed most planting material from European growers. The same problem confronts poor rural households producing snack foods for the urban market in Bangladesh. Preferences change, often quite quickly, and rural producers must adapt their product to suit. Once again linkages are becoming more important, both to acquire information about changing markets as well as to obtain the knowledge and support to deal with it.

Integrated Nature of Challenges

Innovation challenges typically are integrated for two reasons: first, the improvement of a sector requires coordinated actions at different stages of the value chain; second, innovation not only has to raise profitability but also must comply with social and environmental conditions.

Integration of innovation challenges along the value chain. The industrialization of cassava in Ghana and Colombia is an example of the integrated nature of innovation challenges. Industrialization required processing and drying innovations to convert cassava into starch or animal feed, cassava varieties more suited to processing, more efficient agronomic practices, new organizational forms to connect smallholder-based production systems with processing plants, and new financial instruments (futures market arrangements, with forward contracts as loan guarantees). These issues had to be tackled in an integrated way, requiring a high degree of coordination between the actors involved.

Integration of social and environmental challenges into the market agenda. Social and environmental issues are increasingly integrated into the market agenda. Sectors need to support smallholders, who provide the production base for the industry (pineapples in Ghana, cassava in Colombia). In India, exploitation of the poor, the main collectors of medicinal plants, not only threatens their livelihoods but causes them to harvest from the wild in unsustainable ways. In Bangladesh, there is a risk that the small-scale food processing sector might be pushed out by the large-scale sector, but with the right incentives large companies could draw on networks of small-scale producers and makers of semiprocessed products, a business model that has already been tested successfully in the country. Increasingly, social and environmental concerns are embedded in consumer preferences in global markets. Ethical trading and green production are no longer consumer fads at the fringe but mainstream consumer concerns in European and North American markets. New regimes such as EurepGAP integrate consideration for the environment as well as working conditions. An implication of the integration of social and environmental issues is that companies and governments cannot work, plan, and intervene without interacting with actors engaged with these agendas; a second implication is that they will require new types of expertise to do so.

KEY CHARACTERISTICS OF INNOVATION ACROSS THE CASE STUDIES

> **Characteristic 1: Innovation is neither science nor technology but the application of knowledge of all types to achieve desired social and economic outcomes.**

Most cases were characterized by a combination of radical innovation and continuous innovation, related with several types of new knowledge (table 5.1).

Table 5.1 Scope of Innovations Observed

Sector and country	Radical or initiating innovations	Continuous innovations
Shrimp, Bangladesh	Investment in marine product processing plants by the private sector	Quality and hygiene measures to meet changing standards and norms in international markets; shrimp disease control; production methods
Small-scale food processing, Bangladesh	Shift of poor people to food processing as a new livelihood option	Development of new products to match changing food preferences in rural areas
Medicinal plants, India	Modernization of larger manufacturers of herbal remedies; creation of over-the-counter cures, coupled with packaging and marketing innovations aimed at a new market; recognition that traditional medicine is essential to "health for all"	Initiatives to secure the sustainability of the production base; shifts from collection to cultivation of medicinal plants; mechanism to improve the benefits to poor people (producer-owned companies and revitalization of traditional knowledge system); better regulatory frameworks; industry standard of good practice to improve quality; packaging and marketing innovation by corporate sector; pharmaceutical companies exploring herbal-based remedies; government sector-coordinating mechanisms
Vanilla, India	Adoption of new crop	Formation of farmer association for knowledge sharing and collective bargaining; creation of producer-owned company to improve returns to farmers and develop new domestic market for vanilla-based products; new products (vanilla tea)
Pineapple, Ghana	Adoption of non-traditional export	Introduction of new varieties; measures to comply with increasingly stringent EurepGAP and other standards
Cassava processing, Ghana	Novel use of food crop as industrial crop	Development of production and marketing systems; quality improvement, product development, and improved processing efficiency; research projects with strong participation of market actors
Cassava, Colombia	Novel use of food crop as industrial crop	Organizational changes to link farmers and processors; new financial instrument to give better access to credit to increase crop production; more efficient production and processing technologies

continued

Table 5.1 *Continued*		
Sector and country	**Radical or initiating innovations**	**Continuous innovations**
Cut flowers, Colombia	Adoption of cut flowers as a new crop	Frequent shifts to different flower varieties; foliage plants suited to small-scale producers; switch to servicing the domestic market; measures to introduce labor standards acceptable to European buyers and NGOs

Source: Authors.

The case studies illustrate the diversity of change—unforeseen changes in the production, policy, and marketing environment, as well as intentional innovations to grasp new opportunities or cope with the changing context. Some of these innovations involved the use of agricultural technology; in Ghana, pineapple producers needed to adopt a new pineapple variety because the preference of the main export market in Europe had changed. New drying and processing technologies were among the innovations required for cassava to be used as an industrial raw material in Ghana and Colombia.

Besides technical innovations, marketing innovations have also been important. In the Colombian cut flower industry, marketing innovations to target products at specific celebrations in the U.S. market associated with giving flowers (Mother's Day, Valentine's Day) were crucial. Marketing innovations are not necessarily confined to the organized sector. The marketing strategies employed by poor Bangladeshi food processors, who used country recipes and appealing presentations to attract customers to their products, were equally important. The Colombian industry also used an organizational innovation to support marketing, which was to create an exporters' association, Asocolflores.

Process or institutional innovations—in other words, new ways of working —were also important. For example, deploying a partnership-based approach to food science research was an entirely new way of doing research in Ghana, and it allowed much better technical support to be given to value chain development. Financial innovations were also important in a number of cases. In the cassava processing case in Colombia, a futures-based financing mechanism was used to provide production credits to smallholders to raise production.

All of these different types of innovation were important for success in the sectors under study. They all required the use of knowledge that was new to the organizations involved. Although research was one important source of this knowledge, it was by no means the only source.

> **Characteristic 2: Often innovation combines technical, organizational, and other sorts of changes.**

The innovations required to improve quality standards and to conform to sanitary and phytosanitary standards, such as the introduction of HACCP protocols in the Bangladesh shrimp industry, involved both technical change—new processing techniques—and organizational change—new protocols, auditing procedures, and other documentation—to implement and demonstrate compliance. The EurepGAP regulation brought about similar changes for the pineapple sector in Ghana.

> **Characteristic 3: Innovation is the process by which organizations master and implement the design and production of goods and services that are new to them, irrespective of whether they are new to their competitors, their country, or the world.**

Most innovations observed in the case studies were novel to the user or location rather than to the world. The spread and development of vanilla production and the establishment of India as an internationally recognized vanilla producer were not novel in the global scenario, but certainly they constitute an innovation in the production and marketing activities of Indian farmers and traders. When poor rural households in Bangladesh started producing and selling snack foods, this new livelihood option was an innovation for them, and it featured the novel use of existing knowledge about food processing and marketing. The introduction of HACCP in the Bangladesh shrimp sector represented an innovation in quality management for the sector as well as a novel use of a quality management protocol developed and applied in other countries and food sectors.

These examples point to the potential value of developing extension approaches and modes of organization that reflect the ways that innovation systems work—in other words, that bring people together to demand, share, and use knowledge (box 5.1). It is increasingly evident that innovation often arises from farmers and companies reworking the existing stock of knowledge, rather than from a process driven by a research system. This finding suggests that technical advisory services that provide advice and assistance (for example, to provide specialized technical services or develop sufficient linkages) should play a more prominent role in this process.

> **Characteristic 4: Innovation comprises radical and many small improvements and a continuous process of upgrading.**

In 1999 the government of India, assisted by the World Bank, started to evaluate an extension approach under the aegis of agricultural technology management agencies (ATMAs) operating at the district level. The ATMA approach was developed in response to several concerns:

- The current extension service (based on the training and visit approach) was very costly and difficult to sustain.
- Extension had become supply driven rather than market driven.
- Extension focused on staple food crops and gave little attention to livestock and high-value agriculture.
- Extension gave little attention to organizing farmers.

Each ATMA works within the district as an intermediary organization to link farmer organizations, government agencies, private enterprises, and NGOs. Government officials and stakeholders are equally represented on the ATMA's governing board, which includes a cross-section of farmers, women, disadvantaged groups, and private firms. A key activity of the ATMAs is to organize farmer interest groups at the local level. This strategy has effectively mobilized men, women, and young people to join common interest groups for production (flowers, fruit, vegetables, milk, and other products) as well as marketing. The interest groups have also developed federations for mutual support.

ATMA is a new, decentralized approach that emphasizes agricultural diversification, farm income, and rural employment. Decision making is based on bottom-up procedures that directly involve farmer interest groups, the private sector, and NGOs in planning and implementing programs. ATMAs have supported private extension initiatives by contracting NGOs to assume extension responsibilities, by using farmer-to-farmer extension services provided by individuals or through farmer organizations, by developing partnerships with providers of inputs (seed, fertilizer, crop protection chemicals) for demonstrations and farmer training, and by facilitating contracts between processors and farmer groups.

ATMA success stories include the cultivation and marketing of high-value crops (such as flowers, fruit, vegetables, and medicinal plants); integrated pest management; organic farming; well recharging; and the development of new enterprises (such as cashew processing, beekeeping, dairying, and group marketing). By 2004 more than 250 farmer-led innovations had been successfully implemented. Growth rates were significantly higher in ATMA districts than in non-ATMA districts. The rate of return to the investment in ATMAs was conservatively estimated at 23 percent.

Source: Singh, Swanson, and Singh 2005; World Bank 2006b.

The innovations observed were not just one-off events; they included major changes and incremental improvements. In the case of cut flowers in Colombia, the industry had to switch to the production of different flower types because its main markets continued to change. In Ghana, the pineapple industry had to deal with the introduction of EurepGAP regulations; as they became stricter, the industry had to respond with better protocols. When European consumers began to favor a different pineapple variety, innovations were required in bulking up and distributing planting material to effect rapid change across the sector.

The Bangladesh shrimp case is a catalog of obstacles that the industry had to innovate around over the past two decades: a pathogen that discolored the shrimp, an export ban imposed by the European market because of hygiene concerns, climatic conditions that affected shrimp production, and the tsunami and its effect on perceptions about the quality of marine products from Asia. Innovations were required to overcome all of these obstacles. Furthermore, there is no logical progression from one type of innovation to another. The only certainty is that as sectors become increasingly linked into domestic and export markets, the challenges they face become more dynamic and changeable, and the pressure for farmers and companies to innovate becomes that much greater.

Characteristic 5: Innovation can be triggered in many ways.

The cases illustrate a number of initiating triggers: market triggers, policy triggers, knowledge triggers, and resource triggers (table 5.2). These triggers do not act alone but tend to interact. Growth in vanilla production resulted from a (minor) policy trigger and (major) market trigger. The resurgence in medicinal plants, triggered by the market, took place because of India's traditional medicinal heritage, its rich biodiversity, and its tradition of using and manufacturing herbal-based medicines.

Characteristic 6: Considerable value is being added in non-traditional agricultural sectors.

Data are relatively unavailable for many of the sectors studied, but the available evidence shows that many of them have considerable economic value and contribute significantly to the livelihood options of the poor (table 5.3). In several cases, the economic importance of these quickly growing sectors was above expectation. A parallel may be drawn to the evidence regarding job creation in most countries: most jobs are usually not created through the formal corporate sector but through the establishment of new enterprises that may

Table 5.2 Innovation Triggers

Sector and country	Market triggers	Policy triggers	Knowledge triggers	Resource triggers	Context factors that interact with triggers
Shrimp, Bangladesh	Rise in international demand	None	Awareness of European markets	Construction of coastal embankments	Network of Bangladeshi diaspora
Small-scale food processing, Bangladesh	Changing food preferences associated with urbanization and changing employment patterns	None	None	Search by poor people for alternative livelihood options	Existing knowledge base of poor people and artisans on food processing
Medicinal plants, India	Renewed demand for herbal remedies owing to changing health care practices in Europe and North America (and later in India)	None	None	Rich biodiversity	Local medical heritage (codified) and tacit knowledge in Indian systems of medicine; a tradition and capability in both herbal manufacturing and a strong pharmaceutical industry; emergence of sector coinciding with economic liberalization

Vanilla, India	High world prices owing to crop failure in Madagascar; changes in food labeling laws in North America increasing the demand for natural vanilla	Promotion of vanilla to support crop diversification, but on a limited scale	None	None	Tradition of producing high-value spices; tradition of farmer associations
Pineapple, Ghana	Demand in European market	None	None	Foreign ex-change shortage	A series of export promotion policies
Cassava processing, Ghana	Potential market for cassava-based products	Special sector development programs; new research arrangements	None	None	A tradition of promoting agroindustrialization
Cassava, Colombia	Potential market for cassava-based products	Special sector development programs; new research arrangements	None	None	A dense network of research, training, and farmer and industry associations supporting innovation
Cut flowers, Colombia	Demand and proximity of North American flower markets	None	Identification of Colombia as suitable for flower production	None	Larger landowners with spare land; a tradition of export-based agriculture; a tradition of associative organizations for sector support

Source: Authors.

Table 5.3	Value and Developmental Significance of Case Study Sectors		
Sector and country	**Take-off date**	**Value**	**Developmental significance**
Shrimp, Bangladesh	1980s	US$300 million (2003)	Crop of the poor, employment opportunity for the poor
Small-scale food processing, Bangladesh	1980s	Not available	Livelihood option of the poor; 80% of food processing done by poor households and mainly women; 40 million people involved to varying extents; food of the poor
Medicinal plants, India	1980s	Domestic market size of US$1 billion (2000)	Livelihood option of the poor; 1.5 million practitioners of traditional medicine
Vanilla, India	1990s	US$28.5 million (2004)	Crop of the poor; 100,000 small-scale farmers involved in production and trade
Pineapple, Ghana	1990s	US$15.5 million (2002)	Crop of the poor; employment opportunity for the poor
Cassava processing, Ghana	1990s	US$667 million (2004) for the cassava sector as a whole	The major crop produced by poor rural households; 22% of agricultural GDP
Cassava, Colombia	1980s	US$128 million (2004)	Crop of the poor; employment opportunity for the poor
Cut flowers, Colombia	1970s[a]	US$700 million (2003)	Employment opportunity for the poor; second largest legal export product of Colombia

Source: Authors, integrated from various reports.

a. Flowers are one of Colombia's greatest economic success stories, expanding from US$20,000 in the 1970s to over US$673 million in 2002 (Asocolflores 2003).

then grow to become big. Similarly, the improvement of livelihood options, incomes, and employment opportunities in agriculture will be achieved not only through the traditional staple foods but also through the growth of non-traditional and new agricultural activities.

COMMON INTERVENTIONS AND THEIR LIMITS

Traditional Research Interventions

In many of the case studies, research played a remarkably small role. In none of the cases was a research finding the major trigger for innovation. The limited role of research does not mean that research is not required. To the contrary, in almost all cases the sectors have faced or are facing major challenges requiring research, including the following:

- *Pest problems* in shrimp in Bangladesh and cut flowers in Colombia.
- *Improved productivity and lower costs of production to improve competitiveness,* as seen with vanilla in India, with the shift from collection to cultivation of medicinal plants in India, and with cassava in Ghana and Colombia.
- *Product diversification to address new markets,* including the breeding of new flower types in Colombia, the production of cassava flour in Ghana and Colombia, and small-scale food processing in Bangladesh.
- *Quality management systems, including packaging and compliance with international standards and norms,* in all cases.
- *Environmental concerns,* as seen with the shrimp sector in Bangladesh and medicinal plants in India.
- *Ethical concerns* in the cut flower industry in Colombia.
- *Sector studies for policy and planning purposes* for vanilla in India and small-scale food processing in Bangladesh.

Why has research not been a useful intervention? One reason is the lack of expertise to deal with emerging sectors such as cut flowers. Another is the lack of responsiveness to the specific and dynamic needs of the sectors. Table 5.4 provides a summary of research and other interventions as tools to support innovation.

The Colombian cut flower case shows how these two factors—the lack of expertise and lack of responsiveness—interact. The Colombian Ministry of Agriculture and Rural Development supports research related to staple food crops. Because no flower research took place in Colombia, the emerging flower industry obtained new flower varieties by licensing foreign technology and built up technological mastery through associated alliances. Industry associations created at the time worked on export promotion. Later, under strong competitive pressure, research expertise was required for a local flower breeding program. With no expertise in the industry, and virtually no links to the research community in Colombia, it took a long time for links to develop between the flower sector and the research system.

In Bangladesh, agricultural research has focused on crop productivity—mainly of rice. The public sector has conducted no substantial research on food processing relevant to the small-scale sector, which remains almost totally

Table 5.4 Common Interventions and Their Limitations

Type of intervention	Intervention logic	Address short or long term objectives	Responsible organization	Potential limitations	Case study examples
Research	Adds to the stock of knowledge and technology	Short- and long-term objectives	Publicly financed and executed but could also be privately executed	Can become irrelevant without mechanism for linking to sector needs	Pineapple and cassava in Ghana
Research consortia	Embeds research in relations that articulate sector needs and promote uptake of results	Short-term objectives; contributes to long-term change	Public funding; jointly executed by the public and private sectors	Partnerships are ritualistic; consortia fail to introduce more effective ways of using research	Pilot project in cassava processing in Ghana; cassava processing in Colombia
Industry association	Mechanisms for coordinating activities of companies to deal with sectorwide problems, including innovation	Long-term contribution to the development of innovation infrastructure	Organized by industry but could be publicly supported at establishment stage or capacity-building stage	Only promote limited interaction for political lobbying or marketing activities	Shrimp in Bangladesh; cut flowers in Colombia

			Public or NGO actors		
Technology transfer programs	Technology is the main constraint to innovation and can be transferred irrespective of its context	Short term		Technology is not always the key constraint; technology transfer does not allow for the interaction needed for adaptive innovation	Food processing in Bangladesh; cassava in Ghana
Integrated sector support	Sector development requires a combination of interventions that support innovation, value chain development, and policy change	Contributes to long-term innovation system capacity	Government, jointly with all other actors	Becomes too complicated to manage; governance structures skew outcomes; becomes bureaucratic	Cassava in Colombia
Sector-coordinating bodies	Special organizations are required to coordinate the activities of a sector	Long-term contribution to the development of innovation infrastructure	Individually or jointly funded and executed by the public sector, private sector, or NGOs, depending on sector and country and its institutional setting	Become too complicated to manage; governance structures skew outcomes; become bureaucratic	Medicinal plants in India; cassava in Colombia

Source: Authors.

disconnected from the research organizations. The shrimp export industry has almost no visible connection with the Bangladeshi research system. It has no tradition of using research and has relied on imported expertise and technology to solve emerging problems.

Even where research organizations are working on relevant commodities and topics, research traditions are still poorly suited to contemporary innovation demands. Many of the innovations involve small incremental changes. Obtaining information from nonresearch actors may be an easier way to deal with this kind of innovation than research. Incremental innovations are unsuited to research traditions, in which publications of high-impact findings are a key measure of performance. When small-scale food processors in a small rural town in Bangladesh need research support to improve the shelf life of a new snack food, this need is unlikely to attract attention from research organizations.

There is a need for niche research solutions, many of them in the postproduction sphere related to the quality, packaging, handling, and marketing of niche commodities. Most solutions will require applied research or technical support, which in turn will require decentralized research arrangements. *The importance of technical advisory services that help apply existing knowledge to local situations is fundamental.* The Colombian cut flower case study illustrates a point that seems to apply to many of the other cases—within the private sector, the demand for research is weak, and the lack of openness, trust, and a collaborative tradition makes knowledge-sharing difficult, closing opportunities for building a strong knowledge-base within the country. This problem is self-reinforcing. Weak demand for research means that research organizations have few incentives to become more relevant and attract the sorts of linkages that would help articulate demand for research.

Consortia-Based Research Interventions

The case of cassava in Ghana and Colombia has followed a slightly different pattern, relying on consortia of research and nonresearch partners. In Ghana, after a series of research projects exploring technical constraints to the industrial utilization of cassava, it became clear that a key question was how to develop a value chain and integrate research expertise into it. A long time was spent identifying partners and finding ways to establish effective forms of collaboration, so that food scientists could respond effectively to the needs of actors in the marketing chain. For example, the color of the starch produced by one company caused it to be rejected by the confectionary industry. A food scientist picked up this problem, worked on it, and solved it. At the completion of the project, an informal network of cassava processors and food scientists had developed, with sufficient trust to make further collaboration possible when necessary.

In recent years, Ghana and Colombia have succeeded in developing industrial cassava processing as a result of research. However, the source of this success does not lie in innovations arising from either productivity enhancement or more efficient processing technology and novel processed products. Despite some progress, more results are required to cope with highly competitive international markets. What research achieved in both countries was to establish collaboration between organizations and farmers in ways that brought cassava production and processing together.

Coordinating Bodies

Coordinating bodies are observed in a number of case studies. They have not been universally successful. Success has been determined by (1) the mandate of these bodies, (2) their attitudes and practices, (3) their interaction with other sector support agencies, (4) the recognition that both value chain and knowledge integration linkages must be developed, and (5) an emphasis on partnerships as a key methodology. Box 5.2 gives an example of a relatively successful coordinating body.

Integrated Sector Support Interventions

The case of cassava in Colombia provides a good example of an integrated sector support intervention. This intervention had many facets, including the development of linkages to financial organizations; technological upgrading; experimentation with different forms of collaboration, which was seen as a way of building experience and identifying workable approaches; and policy support for the value chain—cassava was part of the pig and poultry chain. Important aspects of success were the existence of an integrated set of support mechanisms for the value chain development and the knowledge integration needed for innovation.

Technology Transfer Interventions

In the case of small-scale food processing in Bangladesh, the local NGO focused all of its effort on training microentrepreneurs in technical aspects of food processing—hygiene, processing techniques, and the introduction of new products. This training failed to build entrepreneurs' capacity to survive in dynamic markets, because it failed to link them to sources of information about changing consumer demands or sources of knowledge that could help them innovate to cope with changing markets. The lack of credit further constrained entrepreneurs' ability to invest in new production or marketing approaches.

Limitations of Firefighting Approaches

The case studies provide a number of examples of interventions designed to solve particular problems. These interventions undoubtedly led to innovations required by the different sectors, but they contributed little to their capacity to innovate proactively in a continuously changing environment. For example, in

The foundation, established as an NGO with government and donor support, engaged in a range of activities, including ex situ and in situ conservation; conservation research; database development on medicinal plants and the traditional knowledge base; research on strengthening local health cultures; laboratory studies on quality standards for traditional herbal materials, products, and processes; development of educational material; and training and capacity development.

The foundation recognized the need to simultaneously strengthen supply chains and to add value by implementing new conservation measures and quality standards for herbal materials. The foundation has tried to integrate different types of knowledge, for example, combining genetic resource conservation science with the ethnobotanical knowledge of communities. The search for compatibility between scientific knowledge and, for example, ayurvedic systems of medicine has not been without its problems, but dialogue between stakeholders in the two fields will build the trust needed to sustain collaboration and innovation.

The foundation's intervention has been relatively successful. It has initiated major conservation and documentation efforts related to medicinal plants and their uses. It established a community-owned enterprise for procuring and selling medicinal plants to support the rural poor who collect and grow these plants. Finally, the foundation has been recognized by the government of India as a scientific and research organization and designated as a national center of excellence for medicinal plants and traditional knowledge. Certain attitudes and practices of the foundation have been critical to its achievements, including the following:

- An experimental approach of learning by doing
- Continuous evaluation of program performance
- Openness to new strategies and wide participation of staff at all levels in decision making
- A commitment to research and implementation
- An ideological commitment to safeguarding Indian health care traditions
- The adoption of a partnership approach
- A commitment to pro-poor development

A final point is the pivotal role of the foundation's leadership. One person has shaped the vision, attitudes, and practices of the organization and consequently has largely determined how the foundation has articulated its mission and approached its implementation.

Source: Case study on medicinal plants in India.

response to the EU ban on shrimp exports from Bangladesh, the government of Bangladesh and a number of international donors helped the shrimp industry adopt HACCP protocols. Yet the hygiene rules introduced by the EU were just one of a series of quality standards that importing countries were to impose on Bangladesh, and these too are constantly changing. Using technical assistance to address each new regulation does not build capacity to innovate unless it is linked to specific efforts to learn from these experiences and develop networks that can both anticipate changes and bring in the expertise to deal with them as needed.

In other words, firefighting approaches result in ad hoc responses but not in a sustainable capacity to respond. In the dynamic environments observed in all of the cases studies, such approaches will not sustain a continuous process of innovation. Sectors or organizations require an adaptive capacity, whereby they are plugged into sources of information about the changing environment. The other facet of adaptive capacity is that it requires links to the sources of knowledge and expertise needed to tackle a varied and unpredictable set of innovation tasks.

CHAPTER SIX

Toward a Framework for Diagnosis and Intervention

This chapter presents a framework that (1) helps to characterize the circumstances and stage of innovation in a particular sector (by asking, for example, what triggers innovation and which actors are predominant); (2) provides guidance in diagnosing current and required capacity for innovation; and (3) on the basis of the diagnosis, suggests principles and gives examples to guide the design of interventions that could strengthen innovation capacity.

The framework, which is based on the case studies, departs from many of the earlier uses of the innovation systems concept by providing additional guidance on diagnosis (the most common use of the concept) and by adding specific ideas for interventions to develop the capacity of innovation systems.

Following the discussion of the framework, this chapter presents a typology of innovation environments, in other words, the situations where innovation capacity is being assessed and where interventions to strengthen this capacity are to be applied. It then describes how the framework can be applied to diagnose needs and elicit principles and options for intervention. Possible options for intervention are listed in box 6.1 at the end of the chapter.

AN INTERVENTION FRAMEWORK FOR DEVELOPING AGRICULTURAL INNOVATION SYSTEMS

The intervention framework consists of four elements, two pertaining to assessment and two pertaining to intervention.

Assessment elements include:

- *A typology of agricultural innovation environments.* A typology of situations that are likely to be encountered in different sectors and in different countries can help the user rapidly assess the characteristics of innovation capacity in a particular context. The typology described here is based on the *origins of sector development* (was development orchestrated by the government or driven by the appearance of new opportunities?) and the *phases of development* of the sector.
- *Diagnostic features.* Distinctive features of innovation capacity are identified for each phase of sector development. These diagnostic features are derived from the analysis of four key elements of the innovation systems concept used in the analytical framework of this study: the actors, attitudes and practices, interaction patterns, and the enabling environment (described in chapter 2). The discussion of the diagnostic features explains why certain features are likely to impede innovation and identifies promising arrangements that could be built upon.

Intervention elements include:

- *Principles for intervention.* The diagnostic features are associated with a set of distinctive intervention principles to address the characteristic weaknesses of innovation capacity in each phase of sector development. *Principles* rather than *prescriptions* are emphasized, because the specific features of interventions must match local institutional and policy settings.
- *Options for intervention.* Examples of interventions are provided, based on the case studies described in chapter 3.

Innovation Trajectories

Sectors and their innovation capacity are shaped by the particular context in which they emerge and by the ways that this context changes over time. As the case studies have shown, the emergence of some sectors can be orchestrated by government, whereas others can emerge spontaneously, driven by the opportunities that present themselves.

This difference shapes the innovation process in very different ways. First, the pivotal actors that start the process are different—broadly speaking, they are either public or private actors. Second, the factors that trigger innovation are quite different—broadly speaking, they are either policy or market triggers. Because the innovation process has a high degree of path dependency, these initial conditions tend to shape two distinctive innovation trajectories or systems: an *orchestrated trajectory* and an *opportunity-driven trajectory.*

The case studies provide two examples of the orchestrated trajectory: cassava processing both in Colombia and in Ghana. In both cases, public investment in food and crop research and special government programs were used to stimulate innovations that could launch cassava processing industries. In both cases, research organizations played the dominant role. All of the other case studies provide examples of the opportunity-driven trajectory. In these cases, market opportunities sparked the take-off of a particular sector, and companies and entrepreneurs played the dominant role. For example, entrepreneurs in Ghana responded to the demand for pineapple in Europe, whereas poor households in Bangladesh set up food processing enterprises in response to changes in urban food consumption patterns.

The context in which innovation capacity originates usually changes over time. The next two sections describe the characteristic phases of development in orchestrated and opportunity-driven innovation trajectories. Table 6.1 shows where the case studies fit into the agricultural innovation systems typology.

Development Phases of Orchestrated Innovation Trajectory

The *pre-planned phase* describes a situation in which no research or other policy intervention has been made, as new opportunities have not yet been identified. There is a research system, but it will not have identified new priorities. None of the case studies illustrates the pre-planned phase, because the studies focused on emerging sectors, but "pre-planning" would have been the situation in Ghana, for example, before food processing was identified as a priority. Many developing countries are at this stage; their research and other policy interventions focus mainly on traditional agricultural commodities. This stage is essential for building a critical mass of agricultural scientists, but it does not lay the foundation for a sector to take off.

In the next phase, the *foundation phase,* priority sectors and commodities have been identified, and the government supports them through research and policy interventions. This phase is characterized by significant investment in research over an extended period, by the development of technologies, and often by the limited effect of these efforts on growth. While the foundation may be in place for a sector to take off, the patterns of interaction between research, the private sector, and other actors required for innovation do not exist.

Next comes the *expansion phase.* The government now intervenes with projects and special programs to link actors in the innovation system. Such efforts might involve consortia-based research mechanisms (as was the case in Ghanaian cassava processing) or commodity support programs aimed at the private sector. Alternatively, they might involve public–private sector partnerships or the establishment of coordinating bodies (as in Colombian cassava processing). This expansion phase is a time to test a variety of mechanisms for building more productive patterns of interaction in a sector and to identify additional problems arising from interaction with existing attitudes and practices. At this stage well-designed interventions, which build on success and

Table 6.1 Place of the Case Studies in the Innovation Systems Typology

Opportunity driven	Emergence phase	Stagnation phase	Dynamic system of innovation phase
	Medicinal plants, India Pineapple, Ghana Food processing, Bangladesh	Shrimp, Bangladesh Vanilla, India	Cut flowers, Colombia
Orchestrated	**Expansion phase**	**Dynamic system of innovation phase**	
	Cassava processing, Ghana	Cassava processing, Colombia	

Source: Authors.

Note: In the nascent, pre-planned, and foundation phases, no case studies were undertaken.

address bottlenecks revealed by piloting experiences, can lead to the development of a dynamic system of innovation.

Development Phases of the Opportunity-Driven Innovation Trajectory

The *nascent phase* in opportunity-driven innovation systems resembles the pre-planned phase of orchestrated systems in a number of ways. The main difference is that the private sector is more proactive. Companies or individual entrepreneurs have identified new market opportunities, but a recognizable sector has yet to emerge. Many of the case study sectors began in this way. For example, in the late 1970s and early 1980s, entrepreneurs in Bangladesh realized not only that their country was suited to shrimp production but that a lucrative international market existed for the commodity.

In the *emergence phase,* the sector takes off. Rapid growth rates are observed: for example, small-scale food processing in Bangladesh grew by 32 percent per year, and the Ghanaian pineapple export sector grew by about 15 percent per year. The sector starts to be recognized by the government. Growth is driven by the activity of the private sector (mainly) or NGOs (sometimes). The existing knowledge and resources of companies and farmers are sufficient for them to participate in these new markets.

In the *stagnation phase,* the sector starts to face increasing and incremental evolutionary pressures to innovate because of competition, particularly from other countries, and because of changing consumer demands and trade rules. This is the most common situation encountered in the case studies. The private sector is the main player and has little connection with research and other government activities, although the industry may be lobbying the government for support. Prices decline as a result of competition, hygiene standards and norms become more stringent, and pest and disease problems become more serious. Companies and farmers lack the knowledge to cope with these new challenges and lack the patterns of interaction to access this knowledge from others. Hygiene concerns led the EU to impose a total ban on shrimp imports from Bangladesh, for example, and preferences in the main market for Colombian cut flowers changed from carnations to spray roses.

Attaining and Sustaining a Dynamic System of Innovation

The ultimate phase of development in orchestrated and opportunity-driven systems is a *dynamic system of innovation,* which can be established with the right type of support. Now the sector is neither publicly nor privately led but is characterized by a high degree of public and private interaction and collaboration in planning and implementation. These relationships help create an agile sector that responds quickly to emerging challenges and opportunities and delivers economic growth in socially inclusive and environmentally sustainable ways. The case studies include two sectors that are moving toward this dynamic phase (table 6.1). In Colombia, for example, a number of organizational and institutional changes are creating the local research capacity needed for the flower export industry to respond to rapidly changing patterns of competition and consumer demand.

Diagnostic Features

As mentioned, the distinctive diagnostic features of orchestrated and opportunity-driven systems are derived from the four analytical elements of the innovation systems concept explained in chapter 2 (actors and their roles, attitudes and practices, patterns of interaction, and the enabling environment). Table 6.2 summarizes the main characteristics of the four analytical elements in each phase. For example, a key feature of the foundation phase in orchestrated systems is a research system that is well developed but has weak links with private companies, NGOs, and microentrepreneurs. This limited interaction fails to promote innovation and usually arises from a lack of trust and mutual understanding.

Principles of Intervention

The innovation systems concept places great emphasis on the context-specific nature of arrangements and processes that constitute a capacity for innovation. For that reason, principles of intervention rather than prescriptions are emphasized here.

Depending on the context and the development phase of the innovation system, different types of interventions may be considered. Interventions in advanced phases of development typically can build on interventions from earlier phases; the more advanced the phase, the more varied the interventions that can take place simultaneously. *Initiating interventions* allow a transition from the pre-planned phase to the foundation phase. *Experimental interventions* allow the transition from the foundation phase to the expansion phase.

Table 6.2   Main Characteristics of the Four Analytical Elements in Each Phase of Development in Orchestrated and Opportunity-Driven Systems

Analytical element	Orchestrated systems			Opportunity-driven systems			
	Pre-planned	Foundation	Expansion	Nascent	Emergence	Stagnation	Innovation
Actors	Traditional public research organizations and private sector actors	Strong public sector presence; increasing private sector activity	Public, private, and civil society actors; emerging coordinating bodies	Private sector and/or civil society actors active	Primarily private sector actors	Most actors in place, but coordinating bodies still ineffective	Coordinating bodies well positioned to support all main actors
Attitudes and practices	Ivory tower mentality; limited trust	Traditional roles predominant	Willingness for collaboration	Opportunistic behavior (private sector)	Self-reliant private sector	Uncoordinated, independent attempts at supporting the sector	Openness to partnering, collaboration, and inclusion
Patterns of interaction	Very limited interaction between main actors; limited access to information	Limited interaction between the main actors taking place	Interaction well developed within the clusters	Very limited networking	Informal private sector networks; poor contact with research	Collaboration weak	A dense network of interactions
Enabling environment	Generic research and training services available (at the most)	Research and training services in place; limited incentives for private sector activity	Incentives for research, training, and private sector activity in place	Generic research and training services available	Incentives not in place; research, training, and financing sectors disconnected from the sector	Increasing incentives; research, training, and financing sectors still disconnected from the sector	Incentives and resources for research, training, and financial sector participation

Source: Authors.

Interventions that *build on success* or *nurture success* help to move from the expansion or emergence phase to a dynamic system of innovation. *Remedial interventions* are aimed at resolving the weaknesses of innovation capacity in the stagnation phase. Finally *maintenance interventions* are aimed at ensuring that dynamic systems of innovation do not deteriorate. Figure 6.1 depicts the phases of development of agricultural innovation systems, starting from either orchestrated or opportunity-drive systems, and how the interventions interact with those phases.

While diagnosis of the innovation system indicates which interventions may yield the greatest benefits, it is also useful to consider cost criteria, given the budget constraints in day-to-day public sector management. Many of the proposed interventions will not be costly or can be put in place by channeling existing funding (for example, research funds) in a different way. Nevertheless, cost considerations would suggest investing first in the interventions that bring about more sector coordination and governance, because they are relatively cheap and make it possible to create a financial as well as a political base for further investments. It may also be wise to agree from the beginning on cost-sharing mechanisms and how they will be phased in.

THE PRE-PLANNED PHASE IN THE ORCHESTRATED TRAJECTORY

Diagnostic Features

Overview. In the pre-planned phase, new opportunities have not yet been identified. Local expertise is available, but producers and entrepreneurs are not sufficiently linked to jointly evaluate market trends and identify emerging opportunities.

Actors and roles. Public research and training organizations and private sector actors are present, but they focus on the traditional priorities of the agricultural sector. Intermediary organizations that could link actors, broker partnerships, or provide access to new sources of knowledge and information are absent.

Attitudes and practices. Research organizations have an ivory tower tradition. The public and the private sectors work independently of each other, and trust between the two is limited.

Patterns of interaction. Interaction among actors is structured around traditional sectors: research links to farmers through agricultural extension arrangements, there is little or no interaction between research and the private sector, and the private sector interacts with government mainly through political lobbying. The public and private sectors have poor access to information about emerging markets and other opportunities, which restricts them from sharing knowledge about new opportunities.

Figure 6.1   Development Phases of Agricultural Innovation Systems

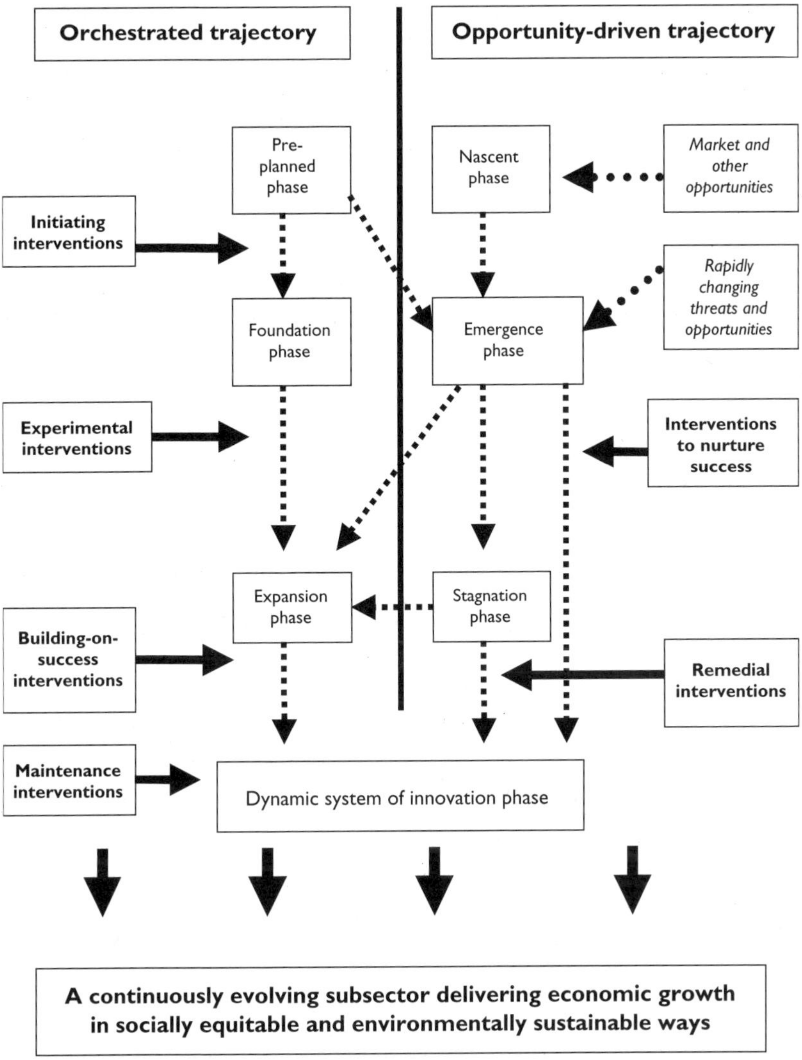

Source: Authors.

Enabling environment. Generic research and training provisions might be in place, but measures in support of a specific sector are not, because the opportunities have not been identified. Financing mechanisms for innovation are usually absent.

Intervention Principles and Options

Interventions are needed to improve the awareness and ability of the existing actors to scan for new opportunities. Interventions should be designed to build trust between the different players. With a potentially large number of different opportunities to choose from, many of which will turn out to be inappropriate, another useful intervention principle is to establish measures to reduce the risk of pursuing new opportunities.

Options for intervention include the following:

- Establish a joint foresight group of industry, government, civil society, and research community representatives to review long-term threats and opportunities for agriculture and to suggest how they can be addressed (1).
- Establish management mechanisms for research and training that allow agribusiness to participate in strategy development, priority setting, and funding (2).
- Provide incentives for the private sector to invest in agroindustrial activities in rural areas in partnership with research organizations (3).
- Establish mechanisms to reduce risks to new entrepreneurial activity, such as tax incentives, grants, or new financing mechanisms (4).

The numbers in parentheses correspond to the specific intervention outlined in box 6.1 (see box 6.1 for a full numbered list of interventions).

THE FOUNDATION PHASE

Diagnostic Features

Overview. In the foundation phase, government has identified new opportunities and set sector priorities. The main tools for stimulating innovation have been investments in research and training, but the sector has not taken off (for example, demand for livestock products may be growing rapidly, but livestock research has not had a strong impact on the sector). The private sector has started to engage in these areas of new opportunity.

Actors and roles. Government and research and development organizations have chosen priority themes or established specific programs. While new technologies may have been developed, they have not been adopted by farmers or entrepreneurs. Entrepreneurial activity is already greater than in the pre-planned phase. Companies are exploring new opportunities identified by the public sector. Intermediary organizations that could link the actors are either absent or weak. Financial organizations do not play an effective role.

Attitudes and practices. Research systems are compartmentalized, hierarchical, and not conducive to interdisciplinary collaboration. The public and private sectors have little trust in one another or practice in working together.

Patterns of interaction. Interaction remains within each sector and does not cross the public-private divide (for example, research agencies collaborate with extension agencies but not with input suppliers). This is likely to be the main constraint to innovation in this phase.

Enabling environment. Primarily supply-driven public research and training arrangements are in place. Incentives for entrepreneurial activity may also be in place, but the financing of innovation may still be a bottleneck.

Intervention Principles and Options

The key principle is to get different actors to work together on specific opportunities and projects identified by the main actors. Interventions should focus on addressing emerging opportunities (existing or new), building trust among the actors, and developing the attitudes and practices as well as financial incentives needed to promote interaction between key players in the sector.

Options for intervention include the following:

- Provide consortia-based research funding to encourage public–private sector interaction on selected priority themes (5).
- Pilot business models based on small-scale producer networks (8).
- Provide incentives for collaboration with foreign agroprocessing companies to expose the sector to different business cultures (9).
- Provide incentives for the private sector to invest in agroindustrial activity in rural areas in partnership with research organizations (10).
- Create farmer associations so farmers can become more effective business partners and acquire knowledge and technology (11).
- Create or strengthen intermediary organizations that can broker and facilitate linkages between poor producers, private enterprises, and research organizations (12).
- Create venture capital funds for rural innovation (13).

THE EXPANSION PHASE

Diagnostic Features

Overview. By this phase, the government has identified a few promising opportunities for meeting such national goals as growth in exports or a reduction in rural poverty. Typical of this phase is a range of time-bound projects and programs, not all of which succeed. This pilot phase is important because it provides an opportunity to find out what sort of arrangements are likely to lead to the emergence of a dynamic system of innovation in different settings of specific sectors and countries.

Actors and roles. Public, private, and civil society actors, each with different roles, have formed clusters, which are typically centered on research or enterprise development. Sector-coordinating organizations, usually established with government support, may be in place. Financial organizations are often not yet included in the innovation system. It is increasingly clear that the main actors have varying capacity to function effectively in their roles.

Attitudes and practices. Pilot interventions have enhanced the willingness to collaborate across the public and private sectors, but the practice of collaboration is still fragile and vulnerable to misunderstandings.

Patterns of interaction. The main actors within the clusters interact, but their interaction still depends on public sector incentives and support. Inclusiveness is still rather weak; for example, NGOs often cannot guarantee the participation of the poor, or an NGO-led cluster-network usually does not link with the corporate sector.

Enabling environment. Funding for research and training is in place. The availability of venture capital and tax incentives for innovation investments may be constrained. The lack of a clear intellectual property rights regime may hinder collaboration and innovation.

Intervention Principles and Options

Interventions should focus on identifying and further expanding the mechanisms and initiatives that have proved to work. For example, if funding for research and industry consortia has been effective, this mechanism may be expanded to new themes or commodities. Interventions should also strengthen existing good practices and address emerging weaknesses in current mechanisms.

Options for intervention include the following:

- Revitalize NGO networks, with a focus on learning and capacity building (14).
- Expand consortia-based research funding for topics where interaction between private companies and research organizations is important (15).
- Provide matching grants to support private sector investments in research (16).
- Create or strengthen a sector-coordinating body with members from the public sector, private sector, and NGOs and representatives from major markets (17).
- Establish training and research facilities jointly sponsored and governed by the public and private sector, perhaps including postgraduate programs (19).
- Change university curricula and involve the private sector in university governance (20).
- Establish internship and exchange programs between industry, universities, and coordinating organizations (21).
- Establish mechanisms for quality and trade certification, and create advisory capacity for achieving compliance (22).

THE NASCENT PHASE IN THE OPPORTUNITY-DRIVEN TRAJECTORY

Diagnostic Features

Overview. In the nascent phase of the opportunity-driven trajectory, entrepreneurs and sometimes NGOs may have started recognizing innovation opportunities, such as new high-value commodities, organic foods, biofuels, or opportunities for transforming traditional sectors. Because local expertise and actors are present, some initiatives result in new markets. However, the government is unaware of these promising opportunities.

Actors. The main actors consist of a small number of producers, entrepreneurs, or NGOs that have recognized new opportunities. Traditional public research organizations may be in place.

Attitudes and practices. The entrepreneurs involved display strong risk-taking and opportunity-searching behavior.

Patterns of interaction. Entrepreneurs have sufficient local links to gain information about emerging markets and other new opportunities but have not developed any networks within the sector.

Enabling environment. Public research and training programs may be in place but are not focused on the new opportunities.

Intervention Principles and Options

No principles or options are listed here, because the need for interventions usually is not apparent until some of the opportunities begin to show potential in the *emergence phase* (discussed next).

THE EMERGENCE PHASE

Diagnostic Features

Overview. Following the lead of one pioneering company or individual, other companies or individuals have gotten involved in the same sector, imitating or perhaps improving on the achievements of the pioneer. At this stage, the sector often relies on low prices as the source of competitiveness. The emergence phase may be short-lived in dynamic market conditions—for example, consumer demand and market standards quickly increase the pressure to innovate. This phase may be brief, but interventions may still be important. Often the networks that could respond to the new conditions through innovation are missing, and the sector may become stagnant.

Actors and roles. The innovation system is dominated by entrepreneurs who rely on their own knowledge and who gain access to new technology and information through their informal networks (friends, relatives in diaspora communities). Technical expertise such as cold chain facilities might be purchased from private providers. Public research plays a traditional, limited role. Farmer and industry associations may have been established.

Attitudes and practices. The business community has no tradition of paying attention to social and environmental considerations, nor has it much trust in or experience in partnerships with the public sector. Quality and environmental standards may exist but are usually unenforceable.

Patterns of interaction. Despite good informal local networks, entrepreneurs hardly interact with the research and policy-making communities. Poor links between industry and research organizations create a vicious circle of weak demand for research and subsequent irrelevant results. As low prices are the main source of sector competitiveness, sector upgrading and creation of a national brand image receive little attention. Where industry associations exist, they focus on lobbying for policy change.

Enabling environment. The enabling environment is usually quite weak. Research, training, and financing organizations do not focus on the needs of the sector. Policy makers are only just starting to recognize the importance of the sector.

Intervention Principles and Options

Interventions should concentrate on bringing the public and private actors together and helping them address the challenges in a collaborative manner. This result can be achieved by developing coordination mechanisms and incentives and encouraging collaborative attitudes and practices in research, training, standards and grades, and brand development. Another intervention principle is to focus on selecting clusters of activities that can receive support for further innovation, in ways that satisfy both economic and social goals.

Options for intervention include the following:

- Provide consortia-based research funding to encourage public–private sector interaction in emerging sectors (6).
- Establish business models based on small-scale producer networks (8).
- Create farmer associations so farmers can become more effective business partners and acquire knowledge and technology (11).
- Create venture capital funds for rural innovation (13).
- Create or strengthen a sector-coordinating body with members from the public sector, private sector, and NGOs and representatives from major markets (17).
- Establish training and research facilities jointly sponsored and governed by the public and private sector, perhaps including postgraduate programs (19).
- Change university curricula and involve the private sector in university governance (20).

- Establish internship and exchange programs between industry, universities, and coordinating organizations (21).
- Establish mechanisms for quality and trade certification, and create advisory capacity for achieving compliance (22).
- Launch product brands based on small-scale processing (23).
- Establish policy dialogues, with public sector, private sector, NGO, and research participation (24).
- Establish a sector-specific research fund governed by sector representatives (25).
- Strengthen NGOs to become intermediary organizations that nurture rural microenterprises, with a focus on knowledge sharing and business skills (26).

THE STAGNATION PHASE

Diagnostic Features

Overview. Many traditional sectors find themselves stuck at this phase, whereas many other sectors that have emerged more recently often quickly enter this phase. Typically, actors cannot innovate around emerging constraints, or they fail to take advantage of new opportunities. A further complication is that there is limited capacity to deal with social and environmental concerns as an integrated part of sector development. Governments and donors are actively involved in trying to support the sector with varying degrees of success, usually addressing problems in a piecemeal fashion rather than building sustainable capacity for innovation.

Actors and roles. Multiple actors have become well established but often entrenched. Entrepreneurs and traditional farmers play a large role. The public sector has recognized the sector and provides support. Civil society organizations may have become active, but they often get mired in a technology transfer role. Coordinating bodies, often established by the public sector, are frequently ineffective. Industry associations (established, for example, to deal with marketing and political lobbying for policy change) may be unable to expand their scope to promoting innovation.

Attitudes and practices. Most actors have become effective in their initial roles but face difficulties in transforming their practices to respond to new situations. The focus of industry associations on marketing or lobbying for policy support restricts their ability to engage in technological upgrading. The regulatory focus of public coordinating bodies restricts their ability to act as troubleshooters. Public research programs are in place but are poorly articulated with the farm and business community; as result, research is often considered irrelevant. Interventions focus on technical assistance and problem solving and less on creating capacity to anticipate and deal with new problems.

Patterns of interaction. Collaboration among the multiple actors is weak. Private sector linkages with the research and training community are still poor;

civil society organizations often act independently of other actors. Even where competitive pressures provide strong incentives for partnership, collaboration does not develop.

Enabling environment. Research and training support and financing mechanisms are in place but are poorly attuned to the emerging needs of the sector. Intellectual property rights protection may have become important to allow providers of new technologies to grow, but a property rights regime is not in place or cannot be enforced.

Intervention Principles and Options

Since the economic importance of the sector has usually become clear, the dimensions of future efforts can be defined clearly. Interventions that build links between the research system and the sector are particularly important at this stage. There is a need for coherent action, among sector actors as well as donors, to address the various emerging technical, environmental, social, and market issues. Thus there is a large role for sector-coordinating bodies that allow the different actors to share their positions and agree on the main issues for development. Since the attitudes toward collaboration are poorly developed, step-by-step approaches, focusing on specific issues and tasks, may be the best way forward. In the long term, this approach will build up the new attitudes that value collaborative ways of working. It is useful to explore options for strengthening the roles of existing organizations—particularly so that they can help promote stronger patterns of interaction—or for redesigning existing research, training, or education programs so that they can become more agile and responsive.

Options for intervention include the following:

- Provide consortia-based research funding to encourage public–private sector interaction in emerging sectors (5).
- Establish business models based on small-scale producer networks (8).
- Provide incentives for collaboration with foreign agroprocessing companies to expose the sector to different business cultures (9).
- Provide incentives for the private sector to invest in agroindustrial activity in rural areas in partnerships with research organizations (10).
- Create farmer associations so farmers can become more effective business partners and acquire knowledge and technology (11).
- Create or strengthen intermediary organizations that can broker and facilitate linkages between poor producers, private enterprises, and research organizations (12).
- Create venture capital funds for rural innovation (13).
- Create or strengthen a sector-coordinating body with members from the public sector, private sector, and NGOs and representatives from major markets (17).

- Establish training and research facilities jointly sponsored and governed by the public and private sector, perhaps including postgraduate programs (19).
- Change university curricula and involve the private sector in university governance (20).
- Establish internship and exchange programs between industry, universities, and coordinating organizations (21).
- Establish mechanisms for quality and trade certification, and create advisory capacity for achieving compliance (22).
- Launch product brands based on small-scale processing (23).
- Establish policy dialogues with public sector, private sector, NGO, and research participation (24).
- Establish a sector-specific research fund governed by sector representatives (25).
- Strengthen NGOs to become intermediary organizations that nurture rural microenterprises, with a focus on knowledge sharing and business skills (26).
- Locate research organizations and enterprises on the same campus (for example, develop agribusiness science parks) (27).

A DYNAMIC SYSTEM OF INNOVATION

Diagnostic Features

Overview. This agile sector responds quickly to emerging challenges and opportunities and delivers socially inclusive and environmentally sustainable economic growth. The sector is not led by public or private actors alone but is characterized by a high degree of interaction among them, including collaboration in planning and implementation.

Actors and roles. Government, private, and civil society organizations all play an active role in the sector. Roles are determined by the nature of the sector and the challenges it faces, and they have evolved over time. Research plays a prominent role, either through strong private sector demand for public research or through privately funded and/or operated research. Sector-coordinating bodies help identify and address technical and organizational issues, including research priorities, quality standards, sector brand image, and trade and policy negotiations. Financial organizations have developed financial products for the sector's specific needs.

Attitudes and practices. There is openness to partnering, a tradition of collaboration, trust between major groups of actors, inclusiveness of poor actors, a strong culture of research within enterprises, and a willingness to take risks. Social and environmental concerns are part of the business culture.

Patterns of interaction. A dense network of interactions links the key actors. These links may be contract based, project based, governance based, or informal.

The network renews and adapts itself in response to new opportunities and challenges.

The enabling environment. Sufficient resources are available for research and training, organized in ways that encourage interaction between organizations. Incentives exist for risk taking, and venture capital is available to promote innovation.

Intervention Principles and Options

Interventions focus on maintaining the health and agility of the innovation system. The system needs to remain well connected to the evolving context. Attitudes and practices need to remain open-minded and collaborative; the enabling environment stays in place. The evolution of the system might bring up new areas of activity requiring new types of research support or new types of organizations.

Options for intervention include the following:

- Establish a joint foresight group of industry, government, civil society, and research community representatives to review long-term threats and opportunities for agriculture and to suggest how they can be addressed (1).
- Locate research organizations and enterprises on the same campus; for example, develop agribusiness science parks (27).
- Conduct detailed surveys to track innovation in the sector and in other countries; conduct knowledge-sharing events (28).
- Develop novel research, training, or financing organizations to pursue new opportunities (7).
- Conduct trade fairs to bring private and public innovation options together (18).

Box 6.1 Numerical List of Interventions, with References to Potential Investment Approaches from the *Agriculture Investment Sourcebook*

The examples listed after each option for intervention are drawn from the *Agriculture Investment Sourcebook* (World Bank 2006a). Although they may provide further insight into potential investments, they were not developed with the explicit purpose of strengthening an agricultural innovation system. Therefore they may need further interpretation and elaboration for use in an agricultural innovation systems framework.

Box 6.1 *Continued*

1. **Establish a joint foresight group of industry, government, civil society, and research community representatives to review long-term threats and opportunities for agriculture and to suggest how they can be addressed.**
   Module 1—Overview: Building Agricultural Policy and Institutional Capacity
   Module 12—Overview: Scaling Up Agricultural Investment in the Bank's Changing Internal Environment

2. **Establish management mechanisms for research and training that allow agribusiness to participate in strategy development, priority setting, and funding.**
   Module 12—Agricultural Investment Note (AIN): Targeting Agricultural Investments to Maximize Poverty Impacts
   Module 7—Innovative Activity Profile (IAP): Colombia: Productive Agribusiness/Farmer Partnerships

3. **Provide incentives for the private sector to invest in agroindustrial activities in rural areas in partnership with research organizations.**
   Module 7—IAP: Colombia: Productive Agribusiness/Farmer Partnerships

4. **Establish mechanisms to reduce risks to new entrepreneurial activity, such as tax incentives, grants, or new financing mechanisms.**
   Module 8—AIN: Microfinance Institutions Moving into Rural Finance for Agriculture

5. **Provide consortia-based research funding to encourage public–private sector interaction on selected priority themes.**
   Module 7—AIN: Private Seed Enterprise Development

6. **Provide consortia-based research funding to encourage public–private sector interaction in emerging sectors.**
   Module 11—IAP: India: Innovative Rainfall-Indexed Insurance

7. **Develop novel research, training, or financing organizations to pursue new opportunities.**
   Module 7—AIN: Food Safety and Agricultural Health

8. **Establish business models based on small-scale producer networks.**
   Module 4—AIN: Smallholder Dairy Production
   Module 11—IAP: Kenya: Commodity-Based Drought Management

continued

Box 6.1 *Continued*

9. **Provide incentives for collaboration with foreign agroprocessing companies to expose the sector to different business cultures.**
   Module 2—IAP: Brazil: Spill-Ins from Foreign Research and Development Laboratories

10. **Provide incentives for the private sector to invest in agroindustrial activity in rural areas in partnership with research organizations.**
    Module 2—AIN: Enhancing University Participation in National Agricultural Research Systems

11. **Create farmer associations so farmers can become more effective business partners and acquire knowledge and technology.**
    Module 7—IAP: Bangladesh: Autonomous Organization for Facilitating Market-Led Export

12. **Create or strengthen intermediary organizations that can broker and facilitate linkages between poor producers, private enterprises, and research organizations.**
    Module 7—AIN: Promoting Private Sector Fertilizer Distribution Systems

13. **Create venture capital funds for rural innovation.**
    Module 7—IAP: Mongolia: Technological Innovation Serving Rural Areas (Khan Bank of Mongolia)

14. **Revitalize NGO networks, with a focus on learning and capacity building.**
    Module 2—IAP: Ecuador: Strategic International Alliances for Capacity Building and Research

15. **Expand consortia-based research funding for topics where interaction between private companies and research organizations is important.**
    Module 4—AIN: Organic Agricultural Production Systems
    Module 5—IAP: Brazil: Participatory Microcatchment Strategy for Increased Productivity and Natural Resource Conservation

16. **Provide matching grants to support private sector investments in research.**
    Module 2—AIN: Competitive Research Funds

Box 6.1   *Continued*

17. **Create or strengthen a sector-coordinating body with members from the public sector, private sector, and NGOs and representatives from major markets.**
Module 1—AIN: Strengthening the Capacity of Farmer Organizations to Influence Agricultural Policy
Module 1—IAP: Ecuador: Commodity Chain Consultative Councils for Policy Formulation

18. **Conduct trade fairs to bring private and public innovation options together.**
Module 7—AIN: Supporting Market and Supply Chain Development
Module 7—AIN: Horticultural Exports from Developing Countries

19. **Establish training and research facilities jointly sponsored and governed by the public and private sector, perhaps including postgraduate programs.**
Module 2—AIN: Enhancing University Participation in National Agricultural Research Systems

20. **Change university curricula and involve the private sector in university governance.**
Module 2—AIN: Local Agricultural Research Committees

21. **Establish internship and exchange programs between industry, universities, and coordinating organizations.**
Module 2—IAP: India: Revitalizing Institutional Capacity in Forestry Research

22. **Establish mechanisms for quality and trade certification, and create advisory capacity for achieving compliance.**
Module 2—AIN: Management of Intellectual Property Rights

23. **Launch product brands based on small-scale processing.**
Module 2—AIN: Biotechnology, Biosafety, and Agricultural Development

24. **Establish policy dialogues with public sector, private sector, NGO, and research participation.**
Module 1—AIN: Adjustment Lending for Agriculture Policy Reform

continued

Box 6.1 *Continued*

25. **Establish a sector-specific research fund governed by sector representatives.**
    Module 2—IAP: India: Focus on Biotechnology

26. **Strengthen NGOs to become intermediary organizations that nurture rural microenterprises, with a focus on knowledge sharing and business skills.**
    Module 12—AIN: Community-Driven Development for Increased Agricultural Income

27. **Locate research organizations and enterprises on the same campus (for example, develop agribusiness science parks).**
    Module 2—AIN: Local Agricultural Research Committees
    Module 7—AIN: Private Seed Enterprise Development

28. **Conduct detailed surveys to track innovation in the sector and in other countries; conduct knowledge-sharing events.**
    Module 2—IAP: Senegal: Making Research Demand-Driven

CHAPTER SEVEN

Conclusions

The agricultural sector of many countries is changing in response to new market opportunities and productivity requirements, new resource management problems, and new roles assumed by public, private, and civil society actors. In this context, the pace of change and level of uncertainty can be considerable. Support to agricultural research and extension systems is necessary but not sufficient to expand the capacity for innovation in agriculture. New ways of enabling innovation are required to deliver economic growth and reduce poverty.

This paper has sought to respond to that concern, and two broad sets of conclusions emerge from the analysis presented here. The first set concerns the nature of innovation and innovation capacities and the corresponding needs for intervention that these findings imply. The second set of conclusions concerns the utility of the innovation systems concept and the resulting intervention framework for diagnosing the needs of innovation systems and designing interventions.

THE NATURE OF INNOVATION: NINE FINDINGS

Finding 1: Research is an important component—but not always the central component—of innovation.

Knowledge created by research is a fundamental building block of an innovation system. The path to using that knowledge successfully in an economy depends, however, on the time and place at which it enters the innovation system. The knowledge created through research can be spatially and/or temporally separated from the innovation system where it is used. The initial success of Colombia's flower sector, for example, was based on varieties and technologies from abroad. As international competition increased, it became clear that Colombia needed to invest in research and technology development to support the floriculture sector. *In other words, the generation and utilization of research results must be coordinated and parallel processes.*

This point leads to another key finding and echoes a similar observation from the manufacturing sector, which is that innovation often involves organizational, institutional, managerial, marketing, or design changes that require special expertise and skills. In addition, successful innovation depends on an array of other conditions, such as the availability of market knowledge, venture capital or other forms of credit, training opportunities, collaborative mechanisms, and policies to enable sector development. Given these requirements, one of the main constraints to innovation is weak interaction between entrepreneurial activity and research.

Research is an important source of knowledge for innovation, but it serves principally as a complement to other knowledge and other activities. Many countries have an urgent need to develop the other elements of the innovation system, particularly more extensive patterns of interaction and the attitudes and practices that support interaction. Once research is better integrated into this wider set of activities, it will become clearer where research capacity is limiting and where it needs strengthening.

This way of thinking reflects a shift in the kinds of interventions that are required. Rather than supporting activities and actors in isolation, such as research and research organizations, or supporting the generation of outputs, such as agricultural knowledge and information, governments should place their emphasis on supporting outcomes that lead to sustainable development through agricultural innovation systems (Hall 2002; Fukuda-Parr, Lopes, and Malik 2002) (table 7.1).

Finding 2: In the contemporary agricultural sector, competitiveness depends on collaboration for innovation.

The context of agriculture is continuously evolving. New regulations, consumer preferences, competitors, pests and diseases, climate change, and human health problems such HIV/AIDS are just some of the changes that agricultural systems may face. Different sources of knowledge are needed to deal with these challenges, which require dense networks of connections. Information may

Table 7.1	Approaches That Link Investments in Agricultural Science and Technology with Progress toward Sustainable Development	
Basis of the approach	**Institutions supported**
Activity based	National agricultural research systems (NARS)
Output based	Agricultural knowledge and information systems (AKIS)
Outcome based	National agricultural innovation system (NAIS)

Source: Authors.

come from public research organizations, technical services in the public and private sectors, development agencies, as well as other entrepreneurs or producers. Many problems cannot be solved by the producer alone; they often require changes in different segments of the value chain. Quality improvement, for example, is as much about production as about postharvest innovation, and it may require collaboration between growers, assembly agents, warehousers, exporters, and shipping agents. Such collaboration is even more important when a sector wants to build a national brand image, which may even require collaboration among competing exporters. Companies need to collaborate to compete, and governments need to be a nurturing partner in this process.

Finding 3: Social and environmental sustainability are integral to economic success and need to be reflected in interventions.

The need to integrate social and environmental concerns can be viewed in various ways.

The supply chain and social and environmental sustainability. In many sectors, small-scale farmers are the production base for an industry (cassava processing is an example from the case studies), whereas other sectors (such as medicinal plants in India) rely heavily on the natural resource base. Creating a sustainable sector requires attention to the "triple bottom line": interventions and policy support must be pro-poor, pro-environment, and pro-business. Attention to social concerns is not important merely to create or sustain a production base. Socially and environmentally irresponsible modes of production are no longer politically defensible. They carry and heighten the risk of civil uprisings, terrorism, and other kinds of economic disruption.

The poor and market sensitivity to social and environmental concerns. Social and environmental concerns increasingly are embedded in consumer preferences in global markets. Ethical and green trade is becoming a mainstream consumer concern in many markets. Companies and governments need to interact with actors engaged with these agendas (mainly civil society organizations). Dealing with social and environmental issues may require new types of expertise and insights into the social structure, asset base, and functions of farming communities, which can guide interventions to bring these communities into innovation systems as partners. It is important to realize that different types of farming communities can exist in the same region or country, and they have varying levels of interest in, capacity for, and resources for creating links with the other actors of an innovation system.

A rule of thumb is that farming communities with a good asset base and access to markets often are more inclined to associate with highly specialized, large-scale, intensive staple crop or livestock production systems, or with innovation systems for high-value products driven by agribusiness interests. Farmers with little land but good links to markets are interested in diversifying production. They may be more inclined to become partners in innovation systems focusing on high-value, low-volume products, especially if sufficient scale is achieved by forming producer groups. Public-private partnerships can be very instrumental in engaging these farmers in profitable enterprises (see the example from China in box 2.6). At the other end of the spectrum are small-scale, resource-poor farmers in marginal areas, where the public sector has a central role to play in supporting social and human capacity building as well as economic activities such as the provision of new breeds and seeds to enhance productivity (table 7.2). From an innovation systems perspective, the priority is to collaborate with facilitators and expert groups who possess deep knowledge of the farming communities and can provide skills and other resources to (1) bring farmers within the realm of the innovation system and (2) adapt institutional arrangements to ensure that farmers—like all other stakeholders—are represented fairly.

Finding 4: The market is not sufficient to promote interaction; the public sector has a central role to play.

The case studies show that even when competitive incentives to innovate are very strong, they are not always sufficient to bring together all of the actors needed for innovation to function or to reach sufficient scale. The public sector's role is important in four ways:

1. To improve patterns of interaction between all relevant players.
2. To provide and enforce an enabling regulatory framework for the differentiated product markets.
3. To support small-scale farmers in becoming partners in innovation systems and in adding value to their assets and skills (for example, through public-private partnerships).

Table 7.2 Innovation Systems and Rural Poverty Reduction, by Type of Farmer and Farming System

Farmer and system type	Innovation system framework	Major actors in the initiation stage
Commercial farmers	- Intensive production systems for nontradable food staples - High-value industries	- Private agribusiness - Public regulatory framework - Producer/trade organizations
Small-scale, market-oriented farmers	- Diversification of production systems - Intensive production of staples to leave land for high-value products - Production systems of high-value, low-volume products	- Public research - Public-private partnerships - Producer organizations - NGOs
Subsistence-oriented farmers	- Staple crops' production systems - Human and social capital building to address a range of livelihood opportunities	- Public research - Producer and community organizations - Women's groups - NGOs

Source: Adapted from Berdegue and Escobar 2001.

4. To provide financing and infrastructure to bring inventions to market (science parks) or to reach a sufficient share of the global market.

Finding 5: Interventions are essential for building the capacity and fostering the learning that enable a sector to respond to continuous competitive challenges.

Dynamic and coordinated interaction among actors in an innovation system often is frustrated by a range of deeply entrenched attitudes and practices that originated when research through a linear process of technology transfer was seen as the main driver of innovation, or when the main source of competitiveness was considered to be low cost (rather than innovation). Such attitudes and practices cause even agile sectors to stall, as occurred in the cut flower industry in Colombia and the shrimp industry in Bangladesh.

The ability to respond quickly to change is an increasingly important element of innovation capacity. For this reason, capacity-strengthening interventions require a major focus on measures that foster strong patterns of interaction and build coordinated action to respond to continuously changing competitive and other challenges. New types of skills must be developed if organizations are to learn from their own and others' experiences of coping with change in a highly uncertain environment. This effort may involve new initiatives (such as technology forecasting or scenario planning) and organizational processes (such as communities of practice to capture tacit knowledge in organizational learning) that can promote knowledge management, sharing, and learning to respond to change effectively.

> **Finding 6: The organization of rural stakeholders is a central development concept. It is a common theme in innovation systems development and in numerous agricultural and rural development efforts.**

At several junctures this paper has highlighted the importance of organizing rural stakeholders. Organization was central to the success of the Produce Foundations in Mexico and the ATMAs in India (not part of the case study analysis). It mobilized innovation in Colombia's cassava and cut flower industries and in India's medicinal plant and vanilla industries. The organization of rural stakeholders is a common element of value chain approaches and community-driven development. Given that investments in organization extend across most development efforts in agriculture (the corollary in irrigation, for example, is the water user associations), they offer important possibilities for synergy with agricultural innovation efforts. Organization can foster two capacities that rural stakeholders tend to lack: the ability to articulate and gain a hearing for their demands, and the ability to negotiate. Investing in rural organizations thus tends to make agricultural innovation systems more effective. Agricultural organization does not substitute for technology, but it improves the ability to articulate and communicate needs for particular kinds of technology, and it increases the likelihood that technology is used.

> **Finding 7: Actors that are critical for coordinating innovation systems at the sector level are either overlooked or missing.**

This study suggests that innovation systems depend on intermediary organizations to facilitate interaction or access to technology and information, and they also depend on coordinating bodies to help integrate the activity of different actors in a sector. There are surprisingly few examples of such quasi-public, quasi-private bodies, which in economics terminology may be described as "club goods." Perhaps these actors disappeared from view in the emphasis on privatization over the last decades, because from a macro point of view their scope of attention is not sufficiently public. From the point of view of an individual actor in a sector, however, such bodies play an important role that benefits everyone in the sector. Commodity boards may be reinvented or revamped to play just this sort of role. It should be observed that where such bodies function effectively, usually it becomes feasible to establish mechanisms that allow them, after initial government support, to be financed by the sector (for example, through a levy or contribution system).

Finding 8: A wide set of attitudes and practices must be cultivated to foster a culture of innovation.

Interaction is only one (albeit important) practice to promote innovation. Innovation capacity is sustainable only when a much wider set of attitudes and practices comes together to create a *culture of innovation,* including a wide appreciation of the importance of science and technology in competitiveness, business models that embrace social and environmental sustainability, attitudes that embrace a diversity of cultures and knowledge systems and pursue inclusive problem solving and coordination capacity, institutional learning as a common routine, and a forward-looking rather than a reactive perspective. In the medium to long term, the development of these types of attitudes and practices will be critical to economic performance.

Finding 9: The enabling environment is an important component of innovation capacity.

The innovation systems concept pays attention to the enabling environment as an important promoter of innovation capacity. This environment often influences how the actors in a sector can put their knowledge to use. The case studies, however, suggest that often the range of actors and the attitudes and practices in a sector constrain the development of sustainable innovation capacity, despite the existence of an enabling environment (for example, an intellectual property rights regime). This finding suggests that policy interventions (for an enabling environment) may often be ineffective if they are not accompanied by efforts to change the prevailing attitudes and practices.

The second conclusion related to the enabling environment is that the ability to agree on the innovation challenges of a sector is much greater when effective value chain coordination is in place. It is thus more feasible to link policy support and innovation efforts and to focus on those enabling activities that actually support innovation. This point once again confirms the importance of sector-coordinating bodies.

THE VALUE OF THE INNOVATION SYSTEMS CONCEPT

Through its explicit attention to development outcomes, the innovation systems concept offers a new framework for analyzing the role of science and technology and its interaction with other actors to generate goods and services. Based on this analysis, an intervention framework has been designed that identifies common weaknesses in innovation capacity in commonly encountered situations, provides principles (as opposed to prescriptions) for intervention, and provides examples of options for intervention.

The value of the innovation concept is illustrated by its power to explain the patterns of sector development in the eight case studies—four representing traditional sectors that are undergoing rapid transformation, and four representing more novel activities. The case studies show that the innovation systems concept can be very effective in identifying the systemic weaknesses in innovation capacity in stagnant (often traditional) sectors and options for creating a dynamic innovation capacity. The case studies also show that this dynamism often depends on the presence of sectorwide coordinating bodies for identifying innovation challenges and facilitating the patterns of interaction needed to enable the innovation process. The cases have suggested a large number of interventions that may help to sustain the dynamism of these sectors, such as the development of farmer associations and the establishment of small-scale producer networks, the establishment of sector-coordinating bodies, and interventions that link research and enterprise organizations and develop the attitudes and practices to sustain interaction. Even though the specific point of departure for the present paper was to examine how the innovation systems concept might provide guidance in going beyond the strengthening of agricultural research, clearly the concept can provide a fresh perspective on agricultural development in general, given its emphasis on the development of partnerships, intermediary organizations, farmer organizations, and other forms of organization and interaction that are critical for development. This versatility suggests that the innovation systems concept may be used to inform other agricultural investment decisions, such as rural credit schemes or private sector development policies.

Although it would appear that the innovation systems concept has something to offer development practitioners, the concept's potential application in agricultural development requires additional empirical validation. In this respect, the analysis described here has contributed to a learning process, similar to the process proposed for building innovation capacity in a sector. Some of the findings are best viewed as hypotheses that need further testing. For example, the typology of innovation environments seems to work for the case studies, but it needs to be validated in other contexts.

This study originated with the proposition to explore new ways of thinking about interventions that could promote agricultural development by better enabling the innovation process. One lesson is that universally applicable blueprints do not exist. Development practitioners must be willing to work with emerging concepts and must recognize that the interventions that they are planning will evolve while they learn.

The findings of the study reveal that an innovation systems approach can promote the integration of poverty and environmental issues with sector development planning by altering the roles and interactions of actors in the public sector, the business community, and civil society. It calls for business actors to develop new patterns of collaboration and governance and to engage in new business models. It calls for public sector actors to assume more of a regulatory and facilitating role, marshalling the resources that enable poor producers to partner in innovation systems. Finally, it calls upon civil society actors to assume a key and responsible role in serving as facilitators between local communities and the other actors in the innovation system. The innovation systems concept provides a framework for inclusive, knowledge-intensive agricultural development, but more experience is required before the contours of a truly pro-poor, pro-environment, and pro-market innovation system can be defined fully.

The innovation systems concept makes two fundamental contributions to designing development interventions. First, it recognizes that initial conditions in a particular country, as expressed in the typologies, largely define how capacity development should be designed. Second, the innovation systems concept emphasizes that interventions should not focus first on developing research capacity and only later on other aspects of innovation capacity. Instead, it suggests that research capacity should be developed in a way that from the beginning nurtures interactions between research, private, and civil society organizations. In other words, countries with research systems may have the potential to leapfrog into more dynamic systems of innovation.

The analysis also reveals the possibility of linking up with previous efforts at capacity development. For example, a country may have invested in scientific capacity and independently built capacity for community-driven development through associations of self-help groups. Each of these capacities has its limitations, but if they are integrated, they might create the interaction needed for pro-poor innovation. Recent discussions of innovation capacity have argued that capacity development in many countries involves two sorts of tasks. The first is to create networks of scientific actors around research themes such as biotechnology and networks of rural actors around development themes such as dryland agriculture. The second is to build links between these networks so that research can be used in rural innovation (Hall 2005). A tantalizing possibility is that interventions that unite research-based and community-based capacity could cost relatively little, add value to existing investments, result in pro-poor innovation capacity, and achieve very high returns.

IMPLICATIONS FOR THE WORLD BANK

With respect to research and extension, the Bank should increasingly look to what it wants to achieve, not to what it wants to support. The traditional research-extension distribution may be exchanged for a model where research supports innovation at the national or regional level and where extension supports it at the local level.

Public research will remain an essential part of the development mix of any agricultural sector, but if support to the public research system allows it to isolate itself from the other stakeholders, this support is money lost. Support to research systems must focus more on developing the interface with the rest of the agricultural sector. Major attention must be given to how and by whom the research system is governed, and to the ability and the attitudes required for engaging in partnerships. Attention must also be given to putting public awareness strategies in place. These types of changes are not necessarily very expensive, but they are preconditions for effective investments in research that can contribute to innovation.

For extension, the implications may be even more extensive. Extension investments should create the capacity to identify new, promising alternatives at the farm level and ensure that they are supported in the right way (for example, through NGOs, by engaging private companies or farmer organizations, or by providing market information). The Bank should support investments that encourage pluralism in service providers and in organizations that have the attitude and the ability to find the right approach in different situations. Investments in such models will by definition be more flexible and less defined in terms of the concrete number of agents or vehicles that will be acquired. To counterbalance the risks involved in such flexibility, governance and accountability should receive additional attention.

With respect to agricultural education, an effective innovation system requires a cadre of professionals with a new skill set and mindset. Technical expertise needs to be complemented with expertise in markets, agribusiness, intellectual property law, rural institutions, and rural finance, to mention a few areas. Above all, this knowledge must be functional—a graduate must be able to apply his or her skills in problem solving, teamwork, group facilitation, and even conflict resolution. The complexity of expertise and skills required puts strong demands on technical vocational and tertiary education establishments. The Bank should reengage in agricultural education investments to modernize curricula, support staff training, and incorporate distance education and other state-of-the-art facilities.

Regarding support to agricultural sector development in general, this paper emphasizes the importance of developing the sector's institutional infrastructure. Intermediary organizations, innovation councils, and the like are central to creating the exchange of knowledge and perspectives that will foster innovation. If their development is handled well, many of these organizations will not be a continuous burden on the sector but will eventually become self-financing and contribute to self-regulation.

The Bank can also bring its investments in community-driven development (CDD) and in agricultural innovation closer, for example by including an innovation fund in CDD loans or by opening a window for CDD and other local organizations in its innovation loans.

The Bank must support more institutional experimentation in addition to the more traditional technological experimentation, especially in poor countries, because it is so clear that often new ways of doing business or of organizing the agricultural sector have been central to success. This conclusion would suggest the value of including funds for venture and risk capital in Bank loans.

A final implication for support to agricultural sector development is to engage private organizations, small and large, more actively as partners with the government in developing and implementing its loans and credits. Such a strategy would first of all help improve the understanding between the different parties, and second would allow a more precise determination of what support is required for agricultural development and where it is required.

Regarding the Bank's position in the dialogue on agricultural development at the global and national level, this paper suggests that the Bank should facilitate the development of a stronger global community of practice in the field of agricultural innovation to further develop and test the innovation systems perspective. While the Bank can take the initiative at first, it would not be expected to have a leading role in the long run. Universities or research institutes may be better suited for this role.

A final concrete step is to collect further experiences from Bank and other projects and to develop operational information on the alternative interventions that have been proposed, including their cost, skill intensity, context dependency, and poverty and environmental effects.

Agricultural Innovation Systems: A Methodology for Diagnostic Assessments

Andy Hall, Lynn Mytelka, and Banji Oyelaran-Oyeyinka, United Nations University, Institute for New Technologies (UNU-INTECH), Keizer Karelplein 19, 6211 TC Maastricht, the Netherlands

This annex sets out the methodology used in the case studies to explain the shortcomings of arrangements used in promoting innovation in the agricultural sector and to identify intervention points for governments and development assistance agencies. The basic hypothesis of the innovation systems framework is that the capacity for continuous innovation is a function of linkages, working practices, and policies that promote knowledge flows and learning among all actors within a sector.

The methodology has been developed for nonexperts or those with limited training who wish to rapidly identify plausible interventions. It describes key elements that must be explored to assess capacity of agricultural innovation systems. Interviews as well as secondary sources of information are used to understand historical patterns of development and to provide the context for the assessment. Although the methodology does not require a systemic survey of actors in the sector of interest, it sets the parameters for designing a survey instrument should it be needed.

More detail on the methodology is available; see Hall, Mytelka, and Oyelaran-Oyeyinka (2006).

SECTOR TIMELINE AND EVOLUTION

Central Message or Diagnosis

What is the nature and dynamics of the sector? Who are the main players? What has been the performance of the sector to date? What challenges does the sector face? How effective have policies and support structures been in triggering innovation and developing a dynamic innovation capacity?

Framework

New sectors or clusters of activity are usually triggered by one event or a combination of events, such as policy or market changes or the intervention of an international development organization or international corporation. There are many types of triggers, and it is important to understand them, because each helps to create a different context in which policies that support innovation must operate. There may also have been a series of turning points in the life cycle of the sector. An awareness of this historical pattern of development and of the local policy and institutional context is vital, because current patterns of activities, roles, and relationships usually have developed incrementally over time.

It is important to highlight that these sectors are evolving and dynamic and that innovation capacities must be able to support their evolution. For example, in Kenya's cut flower industry, many producers actually started out producing green beans for the European market but later switched to flowers. It is important to understand why they had to switch; what resources, linkages, and capabilities allowed them to do so; and how their response was related to local conditions, particularly the institutional and policy setting.

Key Questions

When did the sector start to develop? What factors triggered its emergence? Were these technical, policy, market, or other triggers (for example, changes in trade rules or the opening up of new markets)?

Who were the main players that initiated the sector's development, and what were their characteristics (for example, were they public or private agencies, elite groups of farmers, local or foreign companies, or international development agencies)?

How has the sector grown and evolved over time? Have any major changes in markets, technology, or policy caused it to evolve in new ways? What were the turning points along the way (for example, was there a switch from one crop or product to another, or from the domestic to the international market)?

What other dynamics occurred in the sector? For instance, did world commodity prices fall? Did new, competing countries enter the picture? Did patterns of linkage or capability change in the sector to cope with these dynamics? Or did features of the dynamics within the sector make it difficult for organizations to cope, leading to exit, decline, or alternative paths?

Sector Statistics, Sources of Information, and Methods of Data Collection

Statistics and other information include value, size, growth rate, employment potential, and nature of domestic and international market.

Methods of data collection are secondary documentation; sector investment reviews; earlier studies that have explored science, technology, and innovation policy issues in the sector; and interviews with key informants/sector specialists in the country—considering the importance of triangulating and remaining aware of the possibility of competing or alternative views of how the sector evolved and what was important in its evolution.

SECTOR MAPPING

Central Message and Diagnosis

Who are the main actors and organizations in the sector? What roles do they play, and what are their skills and competencies? Which actors and competencies are missing? Are policies needed to change the role of the public sector or to encourage others to play different roles or play existing roles more effectively? What is the extent of linkages between actors and organizations? What is the nature of these links, and do they support interaction and learning? Which links are missing? What types of linkage need to be encouraged?

Framework

At the heart of the innovation systems concept is the question of which actors are involved, the nature and intensity of their interaction, and the role that they play in the system. Understanding the diversity of actors is particularly important in relation to recent developments in the agricultural sector. Private sector actors and other actors outside government are becoming important players, and public research organizations must reconfigure their roles and relationships in light of these developments.

From an innovation systems perspective it is essential not just to identify links (or missing links) but to unpack these links and see which are working well. For example, if mango exporters are buying expert services from the local university, is that connection sufficient to continuously improve quality and innovate with new packaging or products? Do the scientists listen to the problems of the exporters or just lecture them? Does their advice have any value? How could relationships be improved?

Sector mapping can be split into four parts that involve identifying the existence of relevant organizations, the extent of competency of relevant organizations, the roles of the actors in the sector, and the existence and nature of linkages between organizations relevant to innovation in the sector.

Part 1: Existence of Relevant Organizations
A useful way to identify organizations relevant to a sector is to use Arnold and Bell's typology of actors in an innovation system (Arnold and Bell 2001; figure A.1). This typology has four broad classifications:

- *The research domain* primarily involves formal research organizations producing mainly codified knowledge, mostly in the public sector, but it rec ognizes that the private sector and NGOs may also have a role.
- *The enterprise domain* primarily involves firms and farmers using mainly codified and tacit knowledge and producing tacit knowledge.
- *The demand domain* primarily involves consumers and domestic and international markets for products. It also includes policy actors. Policy actors are not consumers in the conventional sense, but they have a demand for knowledge and information produced by the innovation system (to inform policy), and they should be considered an integral part of the system, just as consumers of more conventional products are.
- *The intermediary domain* involves organizations that may not necessarily be involved in creating or using knowledge but play a critical role in ensuring that knowledge flows from one part of the system to other parts. For example, NGOs, cooperatives, or industry associations might articulate the demand for knowledge or products from disadvantaged or fragmented constituencies such as farmers. This domain could also involve organizations whose business is to broker access to knowledge, including consulting companies or third-party agencies such as those trying to give developing countries access to biotechnology tools.

This typology is far from perfect. The categories are not mutually exclusive. Actors can play multiple roles, and these roles can evolve over time (see below). Nevertheless, the typology provides simple guidance on the sorts of organizations that are likely to be important in a sectoral innovation system. By identifying the range of organizations relevant to innovation in the sector, this initial exercise helps identify organizations that are useful to interview in detail. The interviews will iterate with the mapping exercise.

Sources of information include sector investment reviews; earlier studies that have explored science, technology, and innovation policy issues in the sector; and interviews with key informants and sector specialists in-country.

Part 2: Extent of Competency of Relevant Organizations
Even within the categories of organization discussed above, there will be great heterogeneity. It is important to get some understanding of the competencies that exist within these organizations to gain insight into their underlying skills

Figure A.1   Elements of an Agricultural Innovation System

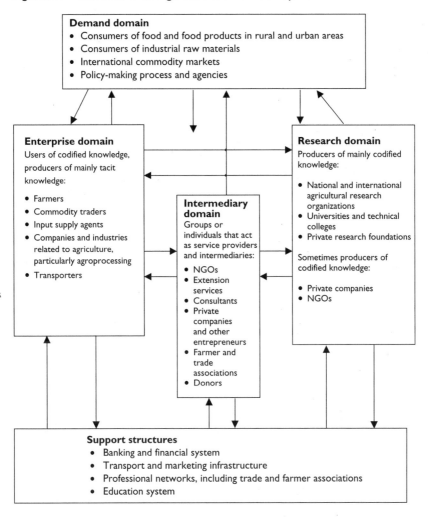

Demand domain
- Consumers of food and food products in rural and urban areas
- Consumers of industrial raw materials
- International commodity markets
- Policy-making process and agencies

Enterprise domain
Users of codified knowledge, producers of mainly tacit knowledge:

- Farmers
- Commodity traders
- Input supply agents
- Companies and industries related to agriculture, particularly agroprocessing
- Transporters

Intermediary domain
Groups or individuals that act as service providers and intermediaries:

- NGOs
- Extension services
- Consultants
- Private companies and other entrepreneurs
- Farmer and trade associations
- Donors

Research domain
Producers of mainly codified knowledge:

- National and international agricultural research organizations
- Universities and technical colleges
- Private research foundations

Sometimes producers of codified knowledge:

- Private companies
- NGOs

Support structures
- Banking and financial system
- Transport and marketing infrastructure
- Professional networks, including trade and farmer associations
- Education system

Source: Adapted from Arnold and Bell (2001, 292) with permission.

and the extent to which these skills can support problem solving, creativity, and innovation. These capacities will include numbers, qualifications, and skills of scientists, managers, and marketing experts. The types of competencies to be investigated will depend on the nature of the organization.

Sources of information include secondary sources, particularly annual reports where available. A systematic sector survey is not part of this methodology;

instead, these questions should form part of a checklist used in face-to-face interviews with key informants. The selection of informants will ensure that different categories of organization are covered adequately.

Part 3: Roles of Actors
One of the features of effective innovation systems is the way organizations beyond the public sector are playing a proactive role in the creation and development of opportunities. In addition, role flexibility is also important, as highly compartmentalized and rigidly defined roles do not allow organizations to reconfigure and respond flexibly to changing circumstances. So, for example, if private seed companies emerge as a major source of plant breeding expertise, should the public sector continue to play this role, or should it adapt and find a new strategic role? If the NGO sector is the major driver of rural development activities, what role should the public sector play? Is the public sector concentrating too much on technology development and not enough on its role in providing supporting structures for innovation, such as credit and training?

Key questions include, Who is the sector champion? Is the champion from the public or private sector? What role are farmers and other sector organizations playing in planning and policy? To what extent are roles in relevant public agencies compartmentalized? How rigid is their mandate? Has this evolved to deal with contemporary development questions? Have reforms defined new roles that have not actually been adopted by these agencies? Are intermediary organizations beyond the government starting to emerge in importance? If so, how are public agencies and public policy trying to deal with this change?

Sources of information include secondary sources, which may include sector studies and reviews of the progress of reform plans in the public sector. More important will be face-to-face interviews with key informants.

Part 4: Existence and Nature of Linkages between Organizations Relevant to Innovation in the Sector
Interactions between actors and organizations are central to an effective innovation system. To understand patterns of interaction, it is important first to map linkages in a general way and then to understand the nature and purpose of those linkages. Two tools are useful for these activities. The first is an actor linkage matrix, which allows the extent of links to be investigated systematically. The matrix is often more useful than a diagram with arrows, which can become too complex and unwieldy. In the actor linkage matrix, all relevant actors in the sector innovation system (identified in part 3 above) are located on both the first row and first column of the matrix. Each box in the matrix then represents the linkage between two actors or organizations. It is important to be *specific* and mention a particular company, producer organization, or research institute rather than mapping linkages between different categories of organization. The example in table A.1 shows that although there are extensive

Table A.1 Example of an Actor Linkage Matrix				
	Crop Research Institute	**Vijay Mango Exports Pvt**	**Krishna farmers association**	**Krishna market commission agents**
Crop Research Institute		Knowledge services contract	Paternalistic	Nil
Vijay Mango Exports Pvt			Input supply links	Input supply links
Krishna farmers association				Output market links
Krishna market commission agents				

Source: Authors.

linkages among organizations, the sorts of linkage that support interactive learning and innovation are absent.

The second tool is a typology of linkages that includes both the type of linkage and its purpose (table A.2). This information is important, as it helps to distinguish between the links an organization might have with an input supplier (important as they may be) and the links it may have for accessing a technology or collaborating on a joint project, which are clearly more important for learning and innovation. This classification of linkages helps to identify the sorts of linkages that might need to develop for continuous innovation to take place. Of the six types of linkage discussed, all may be important in an innovation system at different times. It is more essential to make sure that the right types of linkage exist in the right place. Paternalistic linkages, for example, are of little value where interactive learning and problem solving are required. Successful innovation systems tend to have linkages that support interactive relationships.

It is also useful to classify linkages by the types of learning that they support. The innovation systems perspective recognizes that learning can take a number of forms: learning by interacting, by doing, by imitating (to master process or technology), by searching (for sources of information), and by training. Again, while all of these forms of learning are important, successful innovation systems are characterized by a high degree of interactive learning.

ATTITUDES AND PRACTICES OF ORGANIZATIONS

Central Message or Diagnosis

What attitudes and practices of organizations restrict interaction, knowledge sharing, learning, investment, and exploration of demand issues? What types of attitudes and practices should be developed, and in which organizations? Are

Table A.2   Typology of Linkage and Learning Types

Type of linkage	Purpose	Type of learning
Partnership	Joint problem solving, learning, and innovation. May involve a formal contract or memorandum of understanding. May be less formal, such as participatory research. Highly interactive. May involve two or more organizations. Focused, objective-defined project.	Mainly learning by interacting, but also by imitating and searching.
Paternalistic	Delivery of goods, services, and knowledge to consumers with little regard to their preferences and agendas.	Learning by training.
Contract purchase of technology or knowledge services	Learning or problem solving by buying knowledge from elsewhere. Governed by a formal contract. Interactive according to client-contractor relations. Usually bilateral arrangement. Highly focused objective defined by contract concerning access to goods and services.	Learning by imitating and mastering; might involve learning by training.
Networks	May be formal or informal, but the main objective is to facilitate information flows. Provides "know who" and early warning information on market, technology, and policy changes. Also builds social capital, confidence, and trust, and creates preparedness for change, lowering barriers to forming new linkages. Board objective.	Learning by interacting and searching.
Advocacy linkages to policy process	Specific links through networks and sector association to inform and influence policy.	Interactive learning.
Alliance	Collaboration in marketing products, sharing customer bases, and sharing marketing infrastructure. Usually governed by a memorandum of understanding. Can involve one or more organizations. Board collaborative objective.	Learning by doing.
Linkages to supply and to input and output markets	Mainly informal but also formal arrangements connecting organizations to raw materials and input and output markets. Includes access to credit and grants from national and international bodies. Narrow objective of access to goods.	Limited opportunities for learning; some learning by interacting.

Source: Authors.

policies that are designed to support innovation being negated by existing attitudes and practices? What measures could be put in place to overcome these problems?

Framework

The attitudes and practices of organizations determine their propensity to innovate continuously. Some attitudes and practices affect the critical processes of interaction, knowledge sharing, and learning. Others influence risk taking and determine, for example, whether an organization will invest in the training, new equipment, or technology needed to innovate. Other attitudes define the willingness of an organization to take account of the interests of different stakeholders, especially the poor. Inclusiveness is important to innovation because it is often a source of demand, and nonmarket mechanisms such as collaboration and linkage are important even where market mechanisms are developed.

Attitudes and practices can be very subtle. It is often useful to think about broad attitudes first. For example, is there a tradition of organizations from the private sector working with the public sector, or of research organizations working with enterprise or civil society organizations? What has characterized the relationship between sectors? Is it mistrust? Competition? Apprehension? Disdain?

Relationships within groups of similar organizations also need to be understood. For example, are small-scale agroprocessors accustomed to working collectively and sharing information? Is the competition for donor funds so intense that NGOs compete with each other rather than collaborate?

How do individual organizations interact with others? Using the typology in table A.2, what sort of linkages do they mainly have? Is there a tradition of actively seeking new links and partners, or is the partnership base static? This question is important, because the answer indicates an organization's ability to reconfigure linkages in the face of changing circumstances (in other words, its dynamic capability to innovate). Is the culture of the organization participatory and inclusive or elitist and top-down? How does the organization treat failure—as a learning opportunity or as something to be covered up? Is the organization very hierarchical? A hierarchical structure can stifle creativity and lesson learning at lower levels, or at least prevent them from being noticed or accepted at higher levels where decisions are made.

Do any specific attitudes and practices increase the intensity and quality of interaction with particular stakeholders or client groups, particularly poor ones? In research organizations such practices might include participatory approaches or joint evaluation teams, for example. For companies, such attitudes or practices might also include specific policies to source produce from poorer producers or to employ people from particular social groups. For policy bodies, such a practice might be to commission studies to find out about the agendas of the poor so that their needs can be factored into policy formulation.

Table A.3	Typology of Attitudes and Practices Affecting Key Innovation Processes and Relationships	
Innovation processes and relationships	**Restrictive attitudes and practices**	**Supportive attitudes and practices**
Interaction, knowledge flows, learning	■ Mistrust of other organizations ■ Closed to others' ideas ■ Secretiveness ■ Lack of confidence ■ Professional hierarchies between organizations and disciplines ■ Internal hierarchies ■ Top-down cultures and approaches ■ Cover-up of failures ■ Limited scope and intensity of interaction in sector networks	■ Trust ■ Openness ■ Transparency ■ Confidence ■ Mutual respect ■ Flat management structure ■ Reflection and learning from successes and failures ■ Proactive networking
Inclusiveness of poor stakeholders and the demand side	■ Hierarchies ■ Top-down cultures and approaches	■ Consultative and participatory attitudes
Risk-taking and investing	■ Conservative	■ Confidence ■ Professional incentives

Source: Authors.

How do the attitudes and practices of an organization affect risk taking? Long-established family businesses that have followed the same line of business for many generations are probably less likely to take risks. Strong hierarchies in public organizations tend to stifle risk taking. Professional incentives, such as criteria for promotion, can also affect risk taking. It is important to recognize the existence of these sorts of attitudes and practices, as cushioning policies can be devised to make it easier for organizations to respond to other incentives, policies, and stimuli to interact, invest, or be inclusive. Table A.3 presents a typology of the attitudes and practices that can affect (1) interaction, knowledge flows, and learning; (2) investing; and (3) inclusiveness of poor stakeholders and the demand side.

Sources of Information

Unless specific studies have been undertaken to explore the attitudes and practices of organizations, secondary sources of information are often quite limited. Face-to-face interviews are therefore very important for understanding attitudes and practices. It is useful to remember that because most organizations in a particular country and sector have been shaped by the same historical, cultural, and political setting, the attitudes and practices in the same category of organization will be fairly similar. Scientists in one public research organization may have similar attitudes and practices to scientists in another organization in the same research system. Similarities may exist among feed milling companies, for instance. Although it is dangerous to generalize excessively, broad patterns of attitudes and practices can be found from a limited number of interviews with key informants.

WIDER POLICY AND SUPPORT STRUCTURES

Central Message and Diagnosis

What set of policies is in place to encourage innovation? Which ones are having a positive impact on the behavior of actors and organizations? Which are not? Are there contradictory policies that counteract each other? Do some policies fail to work because of the attitudes and practices of actors and organizations? What additional measures or incentives could overcome this problem? Similarly, are support structures effective? If not, how do they need to be adapted?

Framework

Policies can stimulate innovation by providing the right incentives, resources (including new knowledge from research), and support structures (such as educational or financial system or labor policies). However, policies have to be coordinated: there is no single "innovation policy" but rather a set of policies that work together to shape innovation. Policies must also be relevant to the local context and the attitudes and practices of the actors whose behavior they are designed to influence.

In analyzing an agricultural innovation system, it is necessary to examine the impact on farmers, and others actors, of policies that directly affect the agricultural sector (for example, agricultural research and extension arrangements). It is also necessary to examine the impacts of policies that affect inputs to the sector (for example, industrial and education policies) and the incentives to producers and to companies (for example, tax, land-use, transport, and tariff policies). Finally, it is important as well to examine policies that affect opportunities for learning and competition in the domestic market (for example, intellectual property rights regimes or foreign investment policies).

It is also crucial to recognize that policy changes in the global environment will affect local innovation systems. International market structures and new rules negotiated at the World Trade Organization and other bodies will also shape the parameters within which choices about learning, linkage, and investment will be made.

Other issues are also vital to explore, including the nature of the policy process, linkages between actors in the different policy domains that are relevant to innovation, linkages between policy and practice, and the existence of (and constraints to) policy learning. Box 3.1 presents the checklist of policies that were considered for the niche sectors in the case studies.

Sources of Information

To do this analysis, it is necessary both to understand the goals that particular policies are trying to achieve and to examine how well they are performing. For example, a government may have a policy to promote agricultural innovation by training more students. But if students are not trained in ways that prepare them to work in private companies or development organizations, the policy will have been ineffective for fostering innovation. Information of this sort needs to be collected from relevant ministries as well as through face-to-face interviews with key informants.

ENHANCING AGRICULTURAL INNOVATION

ANNEX B

Case Studies and Authors

A Diagnostic Innovation System Study of the Shrimp Sector in Bangladesh
Zahir Ahmed, Professor of Anthropology, Jahangirnagar University, Dhaka, Bangladesh

The Innovation of the Cassava Sector: The Ghanaian Experience
George Essegbey, Science Technology Policy Research Institute, Council for Scientific and Industrial Research, Accra, Ghana

Innovation of the Pineapple Sector: The Ghanaian Experience
George Essegbey, Science Technology Policy Research Institute, Council for Scientific and Industrial Research, Accra, Ghana

Medicinal Plants in India: Challenges and Opportunities to Develop Innovation Capacity
Rasheed Sulaiman V., Director, Centre for Research on Innovation and Science Policy, Hyderabad, India

Small-Scale Food Processing in Bangladesh: A Diagnostic Innovation System Study
Muhammad Taher, Technology Policy and Development Consultant, Dhaka, Bangladesh

The Story of Vanilla in Kerala—Shifting from Sector Forgetting to Sector Learning

Rasheed Sulaiman V., Director, Centre for Research on Innovation and Science Policy, Hyderabad, India

Strengthening the Agricultural Innovation System in Colombia: An Analysis of the Cassava and Flower Sectors

Lynn K. Mytelka, Professorial Research Fellow, United Nations University–Maastricht Economic and Social Research and Training Centre on Innovation and Technology (UNU-MERIT), Maastricht, the Netherlands

Isabel Bortagaray, PhD candidate, Georgia Institute of Technology, Atlanta, Georgia

Case Study Detailed Summary Tables

Table C.1 Roles of Different Actors at Different Times

Sector and country	Government	Private sector	NGOs	Farmer-owned enterprises, co-ops, and similar
Shrimp, Bangladesh	**Initially:** None **Later:** Policy: Specific sector policies and development of infrastructure (hatcheries)	**Initially:** Started processing factories **Later:** Lobbied government for sector support	**Initially:** None **Later:** Bangladesh Rural Advancement Committee (BRAC) involved in fry production and sale	Role unclear
Small-scale food processing, Bangladesh	**Initially:** None **Later:** Policies tended to support large-scale sector (with no incentives to use local agro-products) and to be aimed at export markets	**Initially:** Activities of microscale entrepreneurs **Later:** Some examples of urban enterprises developing networks of small-scale producers in rural areas; product and process development; training in food processing	**Initially:** Training of the poor in food processing activities, with limited success **Later:** Some support for business development skills and access to credit; research on social and technical aspects	**Initially:** None **Later:** Arrong (part of BRAC) developed network-based production and processing arrangements
Medicinal plants, India	**Initially:** Little **Later:** Creation of department of Indian Systems of Medicine; establishment of Medicinal Plants Board	**Initially:** Companies manufacturing traditional products **Later:** Emergence of large-scale manufacturing companies with widespread product innovation	**Initially:** Limited **Later:** Establishment of NGO to act as coordinating body for related rural development activities	**Initially:** None **Later:** An example of a collector-owned company established to reduce exploitation by middlemen

Coordinating bodies	Financial sector	Research	External agents
Initially: None **Later:** Industry associations active in lobbying for political support, but inactive in sectorwide issues such as quality management and technological upgrading	**Initially:** None **Later:** Industrial bank loans to the sector; a specialist lender emerged for financing culture, seed production, feed production	**Initially:** None **Later:** Limited	**Initially:** None **Later:** Assistance from donors (including World Bank) for sector development; EU assistance to help industry retool to meet new hygiene standards
Initially: None **Later:** Food processing association emerging (Bangladesh Agro-Processing Association), but excluding the poor; pro-poor Forum for Food Processing Enterprise Development (FFPED) failed	**Initially:** None **Later:** Limited support from some microfinance NGOs	**Initially:** Limited product and technology development but limited relevance and uptake **Later:** Remains limited	**Initially:** Donors and international NGO promoting food processing as poverty reduction strategy (with limited success) through training programs **Later:** More focus on business development
Initially: None **Later:** Medicinal Plants Board established as a government coordinating body but with limited effectiveness; NGO coordinating body effective, but only in a domain of activity	Role unclear	Dedicated centers under Indian Council for Agricultural Research, but poorly integrated with herbal drug manufacturers and practitioners of Indian systems of medicine	**Initially:** Limited **Later:** International agencies supporting traditional health systems and associated biodiversity; international companies interested in bioprospecting and drug discovery

continued

| Table C.1 | *Continued* |

Sector and country	Government	Private sector	NGOs	Farmer-owned enterprises, co-ops, and similar
Vanilla, India	**Initially:** Limited, despite presence of government body designed to oversee spice sector development **Later:** Main purchaser of vanilla	**Initially:** Main source of planting material in early stages of sector development	None	**Initially:** Farmer associations main mechanism for diffusing production and post-harvest innovations among farmers **Later:** Producer-owned companies important marketing innovation in response to falling prices
Pineapple, Ghana	**Initially:** None **Later:** Export policy support	**Initially:** Main actors in establishing sector **Later:** Main actors in expanding the sector; also role in multiplying and distributing planting material; specialist companies for technical backstopping on EurepGAP	**Initially:** None **Later:** Specialist technical assistance and linkage brokering NGO activity in supporting the establishment of companies with smallholder production base	**Initially:** None **Later:** Pilot producer-owned company established (Farmappine)
Cassava processing, Ghana	**Initially:** Research and policy support, but poorly integrated and relying on transfer-of-technology approaches **Later:** Research better integrated with actors in the value chain, although still much scope for improvement	**Initially:** Limited **Later:** Became an active player in the sector, responding to both market and policy incentives	**Initially:** Active in technology transfer **Later:** Starting to play the role of intermediary organizations	Unclear

Coordinating bodies	Financial sector	Research	External agents
None	Unclear	Very limited research with very limited relevance in agricultural university	None
Initially: None **Later:** Export and industry associations, but playing limited role in sector coordination for innovation	Development finance for company start-ups available	Research and training capacity on agriculture and botany, but limited linkage and relevance to commercial horticulture sector	Specialist companies to proving technical backstopping on EurepGAP
None	Unclear	**Initially:** Strong but poorly integrated **Later:** Pilot scheme to integrate into value chain	None

continued

Table C.1 *Continued*

Sector and country	Government	Private sector	NGOs	Farmer-owned enterprises, co-ops, and similar
Cassava, Colombia	**Initially:** Strong support to farmers in terms of research, technical assistance, organization, marketing, and credit **Later:** Government withdrawal from research and (later still) return to providing support, but as part of consortia	**Initially:** None **Later:** Developed new equipment to improve cassava processing	None	None
Cut flowers, Colombia	**Initially:** Fiscal support **Later:** Encouraged development of *Commercialisadores Internacionales* (international traders) to enable small firms to export	**Initially:** Absent **Later:** Collaboration for exchange of knowledge and plant material with foreign partners	None	None

Source: Authors, integrated from various reports.

Coordinating bodies	Financial sector	Research	External agents
Initially: Absent **Later:** Fostering collaboration among existing actors and identifying organizational and technical bottlenecks that need intervention	**Initially:** Absent **Later:** Source of credit for small- and medium-scale farmers; agriculture stock market fostering the use of forward contracts, through which both buyer and seller commit to a set of conditions for the future commercialization of the product, such as volume, quality, price, place, and timing	**Initially:** Dried cassava chips as an alternative source of energy in animal feed **Later:** Improvement and transfer of varieties, but also a more integrated and sustainable management of the production system	International agricultural research organizations playing important roles throughout sector development
Initially: None at first, but quickly established industry association to help develop markets **Later:** When technical assistance was needed, proved ineffective owing to history as marketing organization	**Initially:** None **Later:** Minimum interest rates aligned with international rates	**Initially:** None **Later:** Starting to play a role in the private sector	**Initially:** Foreign production expertise and buyers **Later:** Tie-up with foreign companies to develop local flower breeding expertise

Table C.2 The Role of Government in Supporting Innovation

Sector and country	Research	Training	Policy/ regulatory framework	Infrastructure
Shrimp, Bangladesh	Fisheries research	Fisheries graduates, but curriculum unsuited to industry	Fisheries and environmental protection policies	Hatcheries
Small-scale food processing, Bangladesh	Little or none	Little or none	Food standards, but rarely enforced	None
Medicinal plants, India	Research centers under Indian Council for Agricultural Research	Dedicated training organizations for Indian systems of medicine	Guidelines for good manufacturing practice	None
Vanilla, India	Very little, at State Agricultural University	Little or none	None	None
Pineapple, Ghana	Production research under Crops Research Institute	Horticultural graduates, but curriculum unsuited to industry	None	Limited capacity to multiply planting material through tissue culture facilities
Cassava processing, Ghana	Production research under Crops Research Institute and processing research under Food Research Institute	Food science graduates, but curriculum unsuited to industry	President's special program on cassava	Infrastructure development to encourage private industry to establish cassava processing factories
Cassava, Colombia	Strong public research support: CORPOICA (national research organization), CIAT, CLAYUCA	Strong training support through CORPOICA	Coherent clusters of policy support around marketing chain	None
Cut flowers, Colombia	None	None	Supported the development of intermediary organizations to facilitate marketing and distribution on behalf of small-scale farmers	Capital-intensive cultivation technologies

Source: Authors, integrated from various reports.

Incentives for private sector investment	Marketing	Sector co-coordinating bodies	Specific pro-poor interventions
None	None	None	None
Export incentives for large, industrial-scale processing	None	None	None
Grants from Medicinal Plants Board, but relatively minor	Agricultural and Processed Food Products Export Development Authority (APEDA), but relatively minor	Medicinal Plants Board, but facing operational problem	None
None	Indian Spices Board	None	None
Export promotion incentives, including tax-free zones	None	None	None
Incentives associated with president's special program on cassava	None	None	Encouraged the development of small-scale farmer associations
None	None	CLAYUCA	Encouraged the development of associations, intermediary organizations to give small-scale farmers access to export markets
None	Linkages forged in the American market	Commercialisadores Internacionales	Encouraged the development of associations, intermediary organizations to give small-scale farmers access to export markets

Table C.3 Interaction Patterns in Support of Innovation

Sector and country	Main types of interaction	Consequences of interaction	Consequences of lack of interaction	Factors shaping patterns interaction
Shrimp, Bangladesh	**Company-to-company,** through sector association, but focused on political lobbying	Skewed policy change	Difficulty in building national quality brand based on sectorwide quality standards	Historical tendency to secrecy and noncooperation
	Technology transfer through donor and government technical assistance projects	Firefighting approaches that solve immediate problems	Strengthened informal networks that develop adaptive capacity to innovate in the long term	Technical assistance traditions of government and donors
	Missing interactions: Public–private sector partnerships		Weak linkages to research; inability to develop industry-wide standards and practices that all players agree to and are willing to implement	No tradition of research-business collaboration or collaboration on enforcement of regulations
Small-scale food processing, Bangladesh	**Technology transfer** through NGO-led technology transfer activities	Technology transfer the main form of support, even though it may not be needed	The poor remaining disconnected from information on consumer preferences and from knowledge needed for product and marketing innovations	Support to the sector started by NGO with technology orientation, which was copied by others
	Top down, through policy formulation process	Sector remaining largely invisible to public policy, so no investments in support of research on food processing		Data collection traditions in government statistical bureau; policy traditionally focused on the formal sectors; political and policy process dominated by vested interests

	Missing interactions: Between business and the representatives of the poor and the environment	Sector developing in socially unsustainable ways	Failure to create win-win, pro-poor business models in the large-scale sector	Weak tradition of integrating social and environmental considerations into business models; NGO mistrust of for-profit organizations
Medicinal plants, India	**Multiactor interaction** through public coordination body; not very effective	Conservation and health care innovations and an emerging sector that start a dialogue on ways of using medicinal plants in rural health care	Many research and entrepreneurial activities remaining disconnected	Compartmentalization of different research themes; public sector working styles in Medicinal Plants Board; ideological and philosophical differences between private sector and NGO sector, and science and traditional medicine; vested interests in exploitative and unsustainable practices
	Multiactor interaction, through NGO with partnership as a core approach, and that is inclusive of public, private, and NGO actors	A series of technical and organizational innovations to make more effective use of health care approaches in rural development program, but failure to adequately include the private sector	Failure to innovate in ways that fully integrate market and social development with environmental protection	Program with partnership as a core approach; differences of opinion between NGO and businesses on the underpinnings of traditional and scientific health care paradigms Lack of trust between main stakeholder groups, and philosophical differences in traditional and scientific health care paradigms

continued

Table C.3 Continued

Sector and country	Main types of interaction	Consequences of interaction	Consequences of lack of interaction	Factors shaping patterns interaction
Vanilla, India	**Farmer-to-farmer** interaction through farmer associations	Good farmer-to-farmer transmission of production methods and postproduction innovations		A farmer tradition of collaboration across social groups and an association tradition established earlier
	Missing interactions: Multiactor interaction and public-private research including farmers		Weak linkages to new sources of knowledge, particularly from public research organizations; lack of integration of different sources of knowledge	Farmers' mistrust of public agencies; public body that could play a coordinating role, but with regulatory rather than facilitation tradition
Pineapple, Ghana	**Companies and the representatives of the poor and the environment,** through export business models that rely on smallholder production	Development of locally adopted, win-win, pro-poor business models		Compartmentalization of public and private actors; weak tradition of collaboration between different companies
	Missing interactions: Multiactor interactions and public-private interactions in research and training		Difficulty in building national quality brand; weak linkages to additional sources of knowledge, particularly from public research organizations; graduate training not matched to industry needs	

Cassava processing, Ghana	**Technology transfer** interaction through research and extension	Development of inappropriate technologies; inability of processing companies to access suitable technology to innovate and compete in international markets		Traditional divide between public and private sectors and lack of research tradition within companies
	Public-private partnership interaction through a pilot project that created a value chain and the linkages needed to integrate research support	Research to solve emerging technical problems		Emergence of new ways of working in research organizations
	Missing interactions: Multiactor interaction		No national-level coordination to innovate in the sector to improve international competitiveness and meet social and environmental goals	Cassava processing sector not yet identified as core sector
Cassava, Colombia	**Public-private sector partnership** interactions through research approaches that encouraged experimentation with partnership and other forms of collaboration	Innovations taking place in production, harvesting, and processing to support industrial utilization		Tradition of collective action in the form of industry and producer associations; tradition of dealing with postharvest issues and working closely with the processing industry
	Multiactor interaction through regional consortia	Building of links to solve organizational and technical bottlenecks		Key research organizations in the consortia that have a tradition of working on commercial applications in partnership with the private sector

continued

Table C.3 *Continued*

Sector and country	Main types of interaction	Consequences of interaction	Consequences of lack of interaction	Factors shaping patterns interaction
Cassava, Colombia	**Company-to-company interaction** through commodity-based associations	Promotes technical upgrading on sectorwide basis; builds links to solve organizational and technical bottlenecks		Strong national tradition of associations
Cut flowers, Colombia	**Company-to-company interaction** through an industry association principally established to work on marketing issues	Develops marketing but not production innovations for the sector		Tendency to secrecy among flower growers, and the lack of a collaborative tradition
	Missing interactions: Public–private sector partnerships in research and training; multiactor interaction		Growers relying on foreign expertise because locally relevant expertise was not developed; no appropriate graduate-level training program	Main mechanism supporting interaction focused on export and marketing, not on research

Source: Authors, integrated from various reports.

NOTES

1. The NARS comprises all of the entities in a given country that are responsible for organizing, coordinating, or executing research that contributes explicitly to the development of its agriculture and the maintenance of its natural resource base (ISNAR 1992).

2. The AKIS links people and institutions to promote mutual learning and to generate, share, and utilize agriculture-related technology, knowledge, and information. An AKIS integrates farmers, agricultural educators, researchers, and extensionists to harness knowledge and information from various sources for improved livelihoods. Farmers are at the heart of this knowledge triangle (FAO and World Bank 2000).

3. For example, see the Web site for TrendChart Innovation Policy in Europe, an initiative of the European Commission, Enterprise and Industry Directorate General, Innovation Policy Development Unit (http://trendchart.cordis.lu/scoreboards/scoreboard2004/index.cfm).

4. For an exception, see Temel, Janssen, and Karimov 2003.

5. For more details on the role of government in the case studies, see annex C, table C.2.

6. The mission of EurepGAP, the Global Partnership for Safe and Sustainable Agriculture, is "to develop widely accepted standards and procedures for the global certification of Good Agricultural Practices (GAP)." See http://www.eurepgap.org.

REFERENCES

Alston, J., G. Norton, and P. Pardey. 1995. *Science under Scarcity: Principles and Practices for Agricultural Research Evaluation and Priority Setting.* Ithaca, NY: Cornell University Press.

Arnold, E., and M. Bell. 2001. "Some New Ideas about Research for Development." In *Partnerships at the Leading Edge: A Danish Vision for Knowledge, Research and Development.* Report of the Commission on Development-Related Research Funded by Danida, 279–319. Copenhagen: Ministry of Foreign Affairs/Danida.

Asocolflores (Asociación Colombiana de Exportadores de Flores). 2003. "Colombia Una Tierra de Flores Con Mucho Corazon." *Asocolflores Revista* 64: 17–25.

Barghouti, S., S. Kane, K. Sorby, and M. Ali. 2004. "Agricultural Diversification for the Poor: Guidelines for Practitioners." Agriculture and Rural Development Discussion Paper 1. World Bank, Washington, DC.

Berdegue, J., and G. Escobar. 2001. "Agricultural Knowledge and Information Systems and Poverty Reduction." AKIS/ART Discussion Paper, World Bank, Rural Development Department, Washington, DC.

Cassiolato, J. E., H. M. M. Lastres, and M. L. Maciel. 2003. *Systems of Innovation and Development.* Cheltenham, U.K.: Edward Elgar.

CGIAR (Consultative Group on International Agricultural Research) Science Council. 2005. *System Priorities for CGIAR Research, 2005–2015.* Rome: Science Council Secretariat.

Chandler, A. D. 1990. *Scale and Scope: The Dynamics of Industrial Capitalism.* Cambridge, MA: Belknap Press.

Clark, N. G., A. J. Hall, R. Sulaiman V., and G. Naik. 2003. "Research as Capacity Building: The Case of an NGO Facilitated Post-harvest Innovation System for the Himalayan Hills." *World Development* 31 (11): 1845–63.

Dosi, G., C. Freeman, R. Nelson, G. Silverberg, and L. Soete. 1988. *Technical Change and Economic Theory.* New York: Columbia University Press.

Edquist, C., ed. 1997. *Systems of Innovation Technologies, Institutions and Organizations.* London: Pinter, Casell Academic.

Ekboir, J., A. Vera-Cruz, G. Dutrenit, M. G. Martinez Vazquez, and A. Torres Vargas. Forthcoming. "Building the Mexican Agricultural Innovation System: An Institutional Assessment of the Fundaciones Produce" [provisional title]. ISNAR Division Working Paper. International Food Policy Research Institute, Washington, DC.

Engel, P. G. H. 1997. *The Social Organization of Innovation. A Focus on Stakeholder Interaction.* Amsterdam: Royal Tropical Institute.

Engel, P. G. H., and M. L. Salomon. 1997. *Facilitating Innovation for Development: A RAAKS Resource Box.* Amsterdam: Royal Tropical Institute.

Fan, S., P. Hazell, and S. Thorat. 1999. *Linkages Between Government Spending, Growth and Poverty in Rural India.* IFPRI Research Report 110. International Food Policy Research Institute, Washington, DC.

Fan, S., L. Zhang, and X. Zhang. 2002. *Growth Inequality and Poverty in Rural China: The Role of Public Investments.* IFPRI Research Report 125. International Food Policy Research Institute, Washington, DC.

FAO (Food and Agriculture Organization). 2004. *The Market for Non-Traditional Agricultural Exports.* Rome: FAO.

FAO, and World Bank. 2000. *Agricultural Knowledge and Information Systems for Rural Development: Strategic Vision and Guiding Principles.* Rome and Washington, DC: FAO and World Bank.

FAOSTAT (FAO Statistical Databases). 2002. Production yield data on oilseed, cereals, tea, and milk. Accessed at http://apps.fao.o rg/default.htm on May 1, 2006.

Freeman, C. 1987. *Technology Policy and Economic Performance: Lessons from Japan.* London: Pinter.

Fukuda-Parr, S., C. Lopes, and K. Malik, eds. 2002. *Capacity for Development: New Solutions to Old Problems.* New York: United Nations Development Programme; London: Earthscan.

Goel, V. K. ed., E. Koryukin, M. Bhatia, and P. Agarwal. 2004. "Innovation Systems: World Bank Support of Science and Technology Development." World Bank Working Paper 32, World Bank, Washington, DC.

Guinet, J. 2004. "The Rise of An Innovation-Led Growth Model: Implications for Policy in Leading and Catching-Up Economies." Background paper for "Uruguay Sources of Growth." World Bank, Regional Office for Latin America and the Caribbean, Washington, DC.

Hall, A. J. 2002. "Innovation Systems and Capacity Development: Agenda for North-South Research Collaboration?" *International Journal of Technology Management and Sustainable Development* 1 (3): 146–52.

———. 2005. "Capacity Development for Agricultural Biotechnology in Developing Countries: An Innovation Systems View of What It Is and How to Develop It." *Journal of International Development* 19 (5): 611–30.

———. 2006. "Public-Private Sector Partnerships in a System of Agricultural Innovation: Concepts and Challenges." *International Journal of Technology Management and Sustainable Development* 5 (1).

Hall, A. J., L. K. Mytelka, and B. Oyelaran-Oyeyinka. 2006. "Concepts and Guidelines for Diagnostic Assessments of Agricultural Innovation Capacity." UNU-MERIT Working Paper 2006-017. United Nations University–Maastricht Economic and Social Research and Training Centre on Innovation and Technology, Maastricht.

Hall, A. J., L. Mytelka, and B. Oyeyinka. 2004. *Innovation Systems: Concepts and Implications for Agricultural Research Policy and Practice*. Maastricht: United Nations University.

Hall, A. J., M. V. K. Sivamohan, N. Clark, S. Taylor, and G. Bockett. 2001. "Why Research Partnerships Really Matter: Innovation Theory, Institutional Arrangements, and Implications for Developing New Technology for the Poor." *World Development* 29 (5): 783–97.

ISNAR (International Service for National Agricultural Research). 1992. *Service through Partnership: ISNAR's Strategy for the 1990s*. The Hague: ISNAR.

Janssen, W., and T. Braunschweig. 2003. *Trends in the Organization and Financing of Agricultural Research in Developed Countries: Implications for Developing Countries*. ISNAR Research Report no. 22. International Service for National Agricultural Research (ISNAR), The Hague.

Katz, J. 2006. "Salmon Farming in Chile." In *Technology, Adaptations, and Exports: How Some Developing Countries Got It Right*, ed. V. Chandra and S. Kolavalli. Washington, DC: World Bank.

Lundvall, B.-Å., ed. 1992. *National Systems of Innovation: Towards a Theory of Innovation and Interactive Learning*. London: Pinter.

Maxwell, S., and R. Slater, eds. 2003. "Food Policy Old and New." *Development Policy Review* 21 (5/6): 531–53.

Mytelka, L. K. 1987. "Changements technologiques et nouvelles formes de la concurrence dans l'industrie textile et de l'habillement." *Économie Prospective Internationale, Revue du CEPII* 31: 5–28.

———. 1999. "Competition, Innovation, and Competitiveness: A Framework for Analysis." In *Competition, Innovation, and Competitiveness in Developing Countries*, ed. L. K. Mytelka, 15–27. Paris: Organization for Economic Cooperation and Development (OECD).

———. 2000. "Local Systems of Innovation in a Globalised World Economy." *Industry and Innovation* 7 (1): 15–32.

———. 2004a. "Catching Up in New Wave Technologies." *Oxford Development Studies* 32 (3): 389–405.

———. 2004b. "Clustering, Long-Distance Partnerships, and the SME: A Study of the French Biotechnology Sector." *International Journal of Technology Management* 27 (8): 791–808.

Mytelka, L. K., and F. Farinelli. 2003. "From Local Clusters to Innovation Systems." In *Systems of Innovation and Development*, ed. J. E. Cassiolato, H. M. M. Lastres, and M. L. Maciel, 249–72. Cheltenham, U.K.: Edward Elgar.

Naik, G. 2006. "Closing the Yield Gap in Production Technology: Maize in India." In *Technology, Adaptations, and Exports: How Some Developing Countries Got It Right*, ed. V. Chandra and S. Kolavalli. Washington, DC: World Bank.

Nelson, R. 1993. *National Innovation Systems. A Comparative Analysis*. Oxford: Oxford University Press.

OECD (Organisation for Economic Co-operation and Development). 1997. *National Innovation Systems*. Paris: OECD.

———. 2001. *Science, Technology, and Industry Outlook—Drivers of Growth: Information Technology, Innovation, and Entrepreneurship*. Paris: OECD.

Rajalahti, R., J. Woelcke, and E. Pehu. 2005. "Development of Research Systems to Support the Changing Agricultural Sector." Agriculture and Rural Development Discussion Paper 14. World Bank, Washington, DC.

Rosenberg, N. 1976. *Perspectives on Technology.* Cambridge: Cambridge University Press.

Singh, J. P., B. E. Swanson, and K. M. Singh. 2005. "Developing a Decentralized, Market-Driven Extension System in India: The ATMA Model." Photocopy, South Asia Region, World Bank, Washington, DC.

Temel, T., W. Janssen, and F. Karimov. 2003. "Systems Analysis by Graphic Theoretical Techniques: Assessment of the Agricultural Innovation System of Azerbaijan." *Agricultural Systems* 77 (2): 91–116.

Thirtle, C., L. Lin, and J. Piesse. 2003. "The Impact of Research-Led Agriculture Productivity Growth on Poverty Reduction in Africa, Asia and Latin America." *World Development* 31 (12): 1959–75.

TrendChart: Innovation Policy in Europe. 2004. Innovation Scoreboard 2004. An initiative of the European Commission, Enterprise and Industry Directorate General, Innovation Policy Development Unit. http://trendchart.cordis.lu/scoreboards/score board2004/index.cfm.

Wong, P.-K. 1999. "National Innovation Systems for Rapid Technological Catch-Up: An Analytical Framework and a Comparative Analysis of Korea, Taiwan, and Singapore." Paper presented at the DRUID Summer Conference, Rebild, Denmark, June 9–12, 1999.

World Bank. 2002. "Community Driven Development: Broadening Community Authority and Control Over Decisions and Resources." Brochure. Washington, DC.

———. 2005. *Agricultural Growth for the Poor: An Agenda for Development.* Washington, DC: World Bank.

———. 2006a. *Agriculture Investment Sourcebook.* Washington, DC: World Bank.

———. 2006b. *National Agricultural Technology Project: Implementation and Completion Report.* Washington, DC: World Bank.

INDEX

actor linkage matrix, 122
actors, 59, 132t–137t
  attitudes and practices, 48–54
  characteristics by development
    phase, 89t
  Colombia cassava study, 45
  coordinating bodies, 110–111
  cut flowers study, 46–47
  food processing study, 38
  Ghana cassava study, 43
  international, 53–54
  medicinal plants study, 39
  pineapple study, 42
  and roles, 19
    case studies, 62t–65t
    development phases, 90, 92–97, 99
    flexibility, 122
    sector mapping, 120, 122
  sector mapping, 119
  vanilla study, 40–41
adaptability, 109
adaptive capacity, 83
advisory services, 50–51, 80
advocacy linkages, 124t
agricultural development, 1, 3–4, 114,
    xiii, xxi

agricultural education, 114, xxi
agricultural innovation, 66–68, 72b, xiv
agricultural innovation system, 30–31,
    121f
  development phases, 91f
agricultural knowledge and informa-
    tion systems (AKIS), 4b, 6,
    28–30, 107t, 145n, xiv
  features, 27t
agricultural technology management
    agencies (ATMAs), 72b
agriculture, 7–8, 35
  new, 9–10
alliances, 22, 26b, 66, 77, 124t
analysis, 62t–65t, xvi–xvii. *See also*
    comparative analysis
analytical framework, 48, xv
approaches, 5–8, 6b, 81, 83, 107t
ASCo (Ayensu Starch Company
    Limited), 43
Asocolflores (Colombian Association
    of Flower Exporters), 52, 54
assessment, 85, xv–xvi
Association of Small-Scale Cassava
    Farmers from the Cordoba and
    Sucre Plains (APROYSA), 45

ECO-AUDIT
Environmental Benefits Statement

The World Bank is committed to preserving endangered forests and natural resources. The Office of the Publisher has chosen to print *Enhancing Agricultural Innovation: How to Go Beyond the Strengthening of Research Systems* on recycled paper with 30 percent postconsumer waste, in accordance with the recommended standards for paper usage set by the Green Press Initiative, a nonprofit program supporting publishers in using fiber that is not sourced from endangered forests. For more information, visit www.greenpressinitiative.org.

Saved:
- 6 trees
- 4 million BTUs of total energy
- 544 pounds of net greenhouse gases
- 2,256 gallons of waste water
- 290 pounds of solid waste

green press INITIATIVE